THE EASY BAKED DONUT COOKBOOK

THE EASY
BAKED
DONUT
COOKBOOK

**60 Sweet and Savory Recipes for
Your Oven and Mini Donut Maker**

SARA MELLAS

ROCKRIDGE
PRESS

For Melissa, Valerie, Darrell, Ryan, Daniel, Amanda, Anil, and Mavish. I donut know what I would do without your love and support. ⬤

CONTENTS

INTRODUCTION

I was raised in New England, where donuts are an integral part of life: A stop at one of the three Dunkin' Donuts locations in my small town was how I started nearly every day before school for years. There was at least one box of donuts at every social event, and teachers often offered donuts as an incentive for a job well done.

Even having enjoyed thousands of donuts in my young life, and with baking being a big part of my career, it never occurred to me to make donuts at home until I stumbled across a donut pan in a store. I had only ever thought of donuts as being fried, but I knew I had to buy it and try baking them immediately. From the minute I took my first batch out of the oven, I was smitten. Never would I have guessed donuts so delicious could be made so easily, without the mess and hassle of deep-frying. That pan opened a *hole* new world of possibilities that spanned far beyond the breakfast hours.

Welcome to *The Easy Baked Donut Cookbook*! Not only are all the donuts in this book baked instead of fried, they're also easy to make! No matter what kind of donut you're craving, this book shows how you can make it in your own kitchen. The majority of recipes use a donut pan, and some start from homemade dough that you roll and cut into donut shapes before baking. Many can be baked as mini donuts or donut holes or even made in a donut maker.

I've included countless tips, tricks, and recommendations in hopes you'll have as much fun baking donuts as you will eating them! From working with ingredients to accommodate different dietary needs, to playing with flavors to create variations on a recipe, to shortcuts for when you want the least amount of time and effort to stand between you and your donuts, you'll find all the information you need.

There's no measuring cup in the world big enough to measure the amount of joy creating these recipes has brought me. I have a donut-filled gut feeling you will love them as much as I do. Now, set your oven to 350 degrees, grab your whisk, and let's start baking donuts!

MATCHA
GREEN
TEA
DONUTS,
Page 46

1

deliciously easy donuts

Baking donuts is just as the title of this book describes—easy! In this chapter we'll cover everything you need to know to make perfect donuts at home, from getting prepared to bake, to the ingredients and tools you'll use, to simple techniques and strategies for mastering any recipe in this book.

Prep Like a Pro

Whether you are a seasoned baker or stepping into the kitchen for the first time, it's important to set yourself up for success! Here are some of my best tips for being well prepared.

Read the entire recipe: Once you choose a recipe, read it all the way through to avoid any surprises while you're baking.

Take inventory: Check that you have all the necessary ingredients and tools for the recipes you plan to make. If possible, dedicate space in a cabinet or pantry for baking supplies so you'll always know what you have on hand.

Plan ahead: Scan the recipe to see what may need to be prepped—for instance, bringing butter to room temperature, greasing pans, making space to roll out dough—and do these things before you start mixing ingredients. Having everything you need ready and organized lets you focus on one task at a time.

Mise en place: Translating to "everything in its place," this means having all ingredients organized sequentially into separate bowls, and often premeasured, prior to beginning a recipe.

MASTERING MEASUREMENTS

Baking is just as much a science as it is an art, perhaps even more so. Every baked good we eat is composed of a ratio of ingredients that serve a specific purpose, and if those ratios are even slightly off, it can change the final product. One of the easiest ways to guarantee delicious donuts every time is by measuring properly. As opposed to cooking, where an extra tablespoon of butter might make the dish taste slightly richer, an extra tablespoon of butter in a baked donut recipe can prevent the donuts from rising properly or cause the texture to be too dense and chewy. How we measure is just as important as the measurements themselves, and the best method of measuring varies with different types of ingredients.

DRY INGREDIENTS

When it comes to dry ingredients like flours and sugars, the only truly accurate way to measure is by weight. One cup of flour may look exactly the same as another, but the amount of air between the particles can vary significantly.

This can cause your cup of flour to be more or less than what's needed for the recipe, affecting the end result.

For this reason, I highly recommend weighing dry ingredients with a kitchen scale and following the weight measurements indicated throughout. However, if all you have on hand are measuring cups, you can still bake donuts. When you measure, heap your dry ingredients loosely into the cup until it's slightly overflowing, then use a knife to level off the top. For small amounts of dry ingredients like baking powder, salt, and spices, measuring spoons are reliably accurate.

WET INGREDIENTS

Liquid ingredients like water, milk, and oil are best measured with a clear measuring cup that has cup, fluid ounce, and milliliter readings printed on the sides. Be sure to set the cup on a firm, level surface when measuring and read the measurement from eye level. For smaller amounts of liquid like extracts and flavorings, you can use measuring spoons.

For "solid" wet ingredients like butter and cream cheese, measuring by weight using a kitchen scale is the most accurate approach. You can also use the same measuring cups as dry ingredients, but make sure the ingredient is firmly packed into the cup. If you choose to follow the measurements printed on butter or cream cheese wrappers, be sure to do so prior to softening, otherwise, the wrapper might squish the ingredient and skew your measurement!

VOLUME VS. WEIGHT

In the United States, most recipes use only imperial volume measurements like cups, tablespoons, and teaspoons. For the recipes in this book, I list both weight (grams and ounces) and imperial volume measurements, as well as some metric volume measurements (milliliters). As you've read earlier, measuring ingredients solely by volume leaves a lot of room for error, and I encourage you to purchase a kitchen scale to measure by weight. Scales are reasonably priced and widely available online, in department stores, and even in grocery stores. The small investment definitely pays for itself, since you won't waste ingredients on batches of mismeasured donut attempts!

Essential Equipment

It doesn't take much to bake donuts at home. I've included some helpful tools to have in your kitchen. For more specific recommendations, take a look at the Resources on page 155.

Baking Sheets and Donut Pans: You'll definitely need both of these for the recipes in this book. Depending on your preference, I suggest getting at least one 12-cavity or two 6-cavity standard donut pans (3½-inch cavities), two 12-cavity mini donut pans (1¾-inch cavities), and a 20-cavity donut hole pan. I strongly prefer metal pans to silicone, as metal conducts heat much more efficiently, creating nice golden-brown edges on the donuts. For making yeast-based donuts, you will need two large baking sheets, preferably a light-colored aluminum.

Donut Cutters: For any yeast-based donuts, a few round cutters are necessary. You can either purchase an inexpensive set of basic circular cutters and stamp your donuts and donut holes using 3½-inch and 1-inch cutters, or opt for a donut cutter, which cuts ring-shaped donuts in one motion.

Kitchen Scale: As mentioned, kitchen scales are my one true love. There are tons of varieties on the market, but anything that measures ounces and grams and is large enough to be read under a mixing bowl is just fine. Mine cost only $10!

Mini Donut/Donut Hole Maker: These machines resemble waffle irons, but with cavities for donuts. You won't need one to make any of the recipes in this book, but many have the option if you prefer to forgo the oven.

Mixers: A good hand mixer is ideal for frostings and whipped creams. A stand mixer is somewhat of a luxury appliance; it's not necessary but is incredibly helpful when making yeast-based donuts. A dough hook attachment will do all the kneading work for you and improve the texture of soft, sticky donut dough.

Mixing Bowls, Measuring Cups, and Measuring Spoons: A few different sizes of mixing bowls are essential, as are a set of measuring cups and spoons. I like simple aluminum bowls, cups, and spoons, as they're lightweight, durable, and inexpensive.

Paring Knife: My secret weapon! Running a paring knife between the edge of the donuts and the pan helps them pop out easily without breakage.

Pastry Bags and Tips: To easily pipe batter into pans, fill donuts, and decorate, I suggest buying a supply of 14- to 16-inch piping bags, either reusable or disposable. A small round piping tip is ideal for filling donuts. A couple of recipes in this book have the option to decorate the donuts using a large or small open-star tip.

Rolling Pin: Some yeast-based donuts must be rolled out and cut into round or ring shapes. Any rolling pin, wood or metal, with or without handles, will work.

Spatulas and Whisks: In addition to scraping batter from the sides of bowls, rubber spatulas can be used to combine dry and wet ingredients. For mixing wet ingredients or thin batters and making cooked fillings, a good whisk is invaluable.

Wire Racks: Also called "cooling racks," these are ideal for quickly cooling donuts and for glazing. They allow excess glaze to drip off without pooling around the bottom of the donuts.

Love Your Oven

In order to bake the best possible donuts, you have to know your oven. No matter its make, size, or age, every oven performs differently and can have quirks and inconsistencies. Two common oven troubles are inaccurate temperature readings and uneven heating patterns.

An easy way to be sure your oven is truly at the temperature you've set it to is to use an oven-safe thermometer. I recommend keeping at least one, but preferably two, positioned in opposing places in your oven at all times to ensure it is fully preheated and maintains its temperature. Depending on your oven and how many pans are in it at one time, the internal heat circulation can change, causing sections to be at different temperatures. It's important to familiarize yourself with where these areas, sometimes referred to as "hot spots," might be in your oven. This way you can arrange your pans in a place where the temperature reads most accurately, or if using multiple pans, rotate them halfway through the baking time.

If you live and bake 3,500 feet or more above sea level, you'll have additional variables to consider. It is generally recommended to increase all temperatures by 15 to 25°F when baking at high altitudes, but I encourage you to experiment and find what works best with your oven.

Essential Ingredients

One of the many great things about baking donuts at home is that a few simple ingredients can create bakery-quality treats, but it is important to understand how and why certain ingredients are used in these recipes.

Baking Soda and Baking Powder: These leavening agents help baked goods rise and expand. Baking soda relies on both a liquid and an acidic ingredient (like cocoa or buttermilk) to produce carbon dioxide. Baking powder is a mix of baking soda and the acid cream of tartar and needs only liquid for activation.

Butter and Oil: We won't be using any oil to fry donuts in this book, but butter and/or oil are essential for tender, well-structured baked donuts. I use a combination of both for a balance of flavor and moisture. Neutral-flavored canola oil is ideal, but you can also use vegetable oil. Unsalted butter allows for better control over how much salt is in the batter, but if you have only salted on hand, just reduce the amount of salt in the recipe by half.

Chocolate: I can't imagine baking without chocolate, and I use many varieties in my recipes. When it comes to melting chocolate for glazes, ganaches, and fillings, I strongly recommend using chocolate bars sold in the baking aisle of every grocery store. Chocolate chips contain stabilizers that inhibit melting, so save them for adding to batters.

Cocoa Powder: Unsweetened cocoa powder is a main ingredient in all chocolate-based donuts. It is sold in two varieties: natural (non-alkalized) and Dutch-processed (alkalized). For the recipes in this book, opt for natural cocoa powder only.

Dairy: Milk, buttermilk, heavy cream, and sour cream all add richness to baked goods and can impact texture and structure. For optimal mixing, bring dairy products to room temperature before using. While I use whole milk in the majority of these recipes, for cake donuts, 2 percent, skim, soy, coconut, almond, or cashew varieties are all fine substitutes. For yeast donuts, whole milk is essential to the texture of the dough and shouldn't be replaced.

Eggs: Eggs are sold in various sizes, determined by weight. This book calls for large eggs, so keep in mind that using other sizes may alter your results. I recommend bringing them to room temperature before baking, as this helps them mix uniformly.

Extracts and Flavorings: Pure vanilla extract is absolutely worth the investment. Imitation vanilla won't produce the same flavor and often tastes artificial. Extracts like peppermint, maple, and coconut appear in a handful of recipes and are nice to have but are not essential. Fresh citrus zest and espresso powder are two of my other favorite ingredients for boosting flavors.

Flour: For these recipes I use unbleached all-purpose flour. Bleached and/or enriched all-purpose flour are fine alternatives, they are just slightly more processed. Avoid bread flour or cake flour unless specified, as these have higher and lower gluten contents respectively, which can alter the texture of your donuts.

Spices: Spices can be expensive, especially when you need only a teaspoon of something. To avoid overspending, visit the bulk section of a natural foods store, where you can buy the exact amount you'd like. Cinnamon, nutmeg, ground ginger, cloves, and allspice are my favorite spices to use.

Sugars: Granulated sugar, light and dark brown sugar, and confectioner's/powdered sugar are all used here. I like minimally processed cane sugar (not to be confused with coarse granule turbinado sugar), as I find it has more depth of flavor than standard refined white sugar.

Yeast: I use active dry yeast, which is sold in 7-gram packets in baking aisles. It becomes active when mixed with liquid and sugar and requires time to produce the gases that create rise and expansion. It's used for any "raised" donuts or those with a texture more similar to bread than cake.

HOMEMADE HEAD STARTS

Nowhere is it said that being a good baker means you have to make everything from scratch. We purchase butter already churned, so we should be able to buy a box of cake mix or can of prepared biscuits with no shame! After all, the recipes in this book are intended to be *easy* as well as fun and delicious.

A handful of donuts in this book feature ready-made ingredients, like Cake Mix Donuts (page 26) and Easy Apple "Fritters" (page 122). For the best-tasting products, choose labels with short lists of recognizable ingredients. Keep in mind that cake mixes, puddings, and frostings are typically sweeter than homemade versions. Ready-made frostings are also softer than most homemade varieties and are less ideal for any piped decorating.

A Matter of Batter and the Deal with Yields

Whether you choose to pipe or spoon your batter into the cavities of your donut pans, be sure to follow the recipe's instructions for how much to fill them. For most recipes, you'll want to fill your pan's cavities a touch over three-quarters full. If filled too little, your donuts will seem a bit flat and thin, but if filled too much, the batter may overflow, resulting in donuts with cupcake-like edges and no holes.

All these recipes indicate yield, or how many donuts you can expect a batch to make. For yeast donuts, the yield is around one dozen, as proofing, rolling, and the size of your cutters can affect the exact amount. For cake donuts, most recipes yield about 15 standard-size donuts (3½-inch cavities).

One standard-size donut is equivalent to 5 to 6 mini donuts or 3 donut holes. In the recipe yields you'll notice that one batch of 15 donuts is enough batter for 75 mini donuts or 45 donut holes. Unless you're preparing treats for a bake sale or party, that's *a lot* of mini donuts for an average day! With this in mind, you can easily make a smaller batch of any recipe in this book by simply halving all the ingredients (e.g., 1 cup of flour instead of 2 cups, ½ teaspoon of baking powder instead of 1 teaspoon).

Many of these recipes were created to be made at different sizes, so you can use the same batch of batter to make an assortment of standard donuts, mini donuts, or donut holes. You can even bake extra donut batter in a mini muffin pan. Fill the cavities three-quarters full and bake for 11 to 13 minutes.

Essential Techniques

Filling: Most donuts are filled by poking a small hole through either the side or bottom of the yeast donut shell, then using a piping bag fitted with a small round tip to inject filling into the donut. A few of the "filled" donuts in this book are cake donuts, with exposed filling in the center hole. To make them extra pretty, I like to pipe the filling using a large star piping tip, but it can also just be spooned in.

Folding: Folding is a way to combine two mixtures of different textures while allowing minimal air to escape. More intentional than stirring, it involves lifting the mixing spoon or spatula under and over, to maintain lightness throughout.

Glazing and Icing: Some donuts are fully coated in a thin glaze while others are partially dipped in a thicker glaze or icing. Any icing or frosting should go on the top (less browned) side of the donut. If the glaze looks uneven or part of the donut is bare, simply spoon a small amount of glaze from the bowl onto the area. Once all the donuts are on the wire rack, allow the glaze to set for 15 to 20 minutes, or until it has dried.

Piping: I typically recommend using a pastry bag to fill donut-pan cavities with batter; it's more efficient and cleaner than spooning it in. If you don't have a pastry bag, you can also fill a zip-top bag roughly three-quarters full, then snip away ½ inch from the tip of the bag to create an opening. Using your dominant hand to apply steady pressure at the top of the bag and your other hand to guide the tip, pipe the batter evenly into the cavities.

Proofing: Proofing is the process of allowing yeast doughs to ferment and rise before baking. For the yeast-based recipes in this book, the dough is proofed twice: once after kneading, allowing it to rest for 1½ to 2 hours or until doubled in volume, and again after rolling and cutting it into donuts, after which the dough will need to rest for only 30 to 45 minutes. Proofing takes both patience and attentiveness but gets easier with practice.

Rolling and Cutting: Some recipes require using a rolling pin to roll out dough to a specified thickness and cutting it with round cutters or a donut cutter. Use light and steady pressure when rolling, and dust the pin and cutters with flour to prevent the dough from sticking.

Tasty Tips and Troubleshooting

Check your leaveners. In addition to checking the expiration date on your baking powder and baking soda and replacing them every three to four months, be sure to "proof" your yeast before using. Allow the initial mixture of yeast, warm liquid, and sugar to sit for 10 minutes undisturbed. If it is not slightly bubbly and/or foamy after this time, discard it and start over with a new packet.

Toothpick test. Because cake donuts need only a relatively short amount of time in the oven, they finish baking before the tops are fully brown. A toothpick is a reliable way to tell when they're ready. Insert one into a donut. If it comes out clean, the donuts are done. If there's any batter sticking to the toothpick, bake them a few minutes longer.

Have patience. If a recipe indicates freezing, refrigeration, or rising time, it's for a reason! And though it might be hard, let your donuts cool in the pans for at least 10 minutes before removing them to prevent breakage.

Salvage subpar donuts. As mentioned in the "Love Your Oven" sidebar (page 5), no two ovens are alike, so if your donuts appear a bit too brown but taste fine, a colorful glaze or a coating of powdered sugar can hide many imperfections. If your donuts are somewhat overbaked and dry, try sealing them in a zip-top bag with a piece of sandwich bread for a few hours—you'll be amazed at the moisture that can be restored.

Store and freeze. Baked donuts taste best the day they're made. However, baked, unglazed donuts can be wrapped in plastic, sealed in a freezer-safe container, and frozen for one to two months. When you're ready to indulge, thaw them to room temperature before glazing or sugaring. For short-term storage (one to two days), I keep plain or sugared donuts in a sealed container at room temperature, and anything glazed or frosted in the refrigerator.

About the Recipes

The recipes in this book are organized into six chapters: **Basic and Sugared** (plain or coated in some form of sugar), **Glazed** (coated fully or partially in a thin glaze), **Iced and Frosted** (topped and/or decorated with frosting, icing, or a thick glaze), **Filled** (containing some form of filling), **Donut Holes and Donut Desserts** (donut holes, fritters, and desserts made from donuts), and **Savory** (who says donuts can't be dinner?). I've also channeled my love for holidays and celebrations into themed recipes throughout and compiled a handy "Recipes by Occasion" index on page 156.

The recipes include prep time, bake time, and inactive time (for things like chilling, proofing, and cooling). When a recipe works as more than one donut size, the bake time listed refers to the standard size, with specific adjustments for the others noted in the instructions. Many recipes also include **labels** and **tips** to accommodate a variety of tastes, time constraints, and dietary preferences, while ensuring each batch of donuts is a success.

RECIPE LABELS

ADULTS ONLY: These recipes have alcohol, though there are tips to make them booze-free.

DONUT MAKER: These can be made in a mini donut maker or donut hole maker.

HOMEMADE HEAD START: There's an option to use packaged or ready-made ingredients.

MAKE IT MINI: These recipes can be made as mini donuts and/or donut holes.

ONE BOWL: You'll need only a single bowl, which means quicker cleanup. Woohoo!

RECIPE TIPS

VARIATION TIP: I highlight my favorite ways to change up recipes with a simple swap of flavorings, fillings, or toppings.

INGREDIENT TIP: For any less-common ingredients, I note where to purchase and how to use them.

TECHNIQUE TIP: I share shortcuts and little tricks for making donuts extra special (or extra easy).

ALLERGEN TIP: I explain how to alter these recipes to accommodate common allergies and dietary preferences.

TROUBLESHOOTING TIP: We all bake mistakes! I offer advice on how to identify, prevent, and remedy common problems.

CHAPTER

2

basic and sugared

OLD-FASHIONED CAKE DONUTS

PREP TIME 15 MINUTES | **BAKE TIME** 15 MINUTES | **INACTIVE TIME** 30 MINUTES

There are few things in life more enjoyable than an old-fashioned cake donut with a cup of coffee. My best friend insists that a donut shop is only as good as its cake donuts, and I have to agree. The crisp golden exteriors and soft, slightly crumbly interiors are a pure and simple pleasure. These baked donuts could not be easier to make and are perfect when you're craving something uncomplicated and classic.

MAKES

15 DONUTS

75 MINI DONUTS

45 DONUT HOLES

DONUT MAKER

MAKE IT MINI

ONE BOWL

Nonstick cooking spray
6 tablespoons (84g) unsalted butter, melted
4 teaspoons (20ml) canola oil
¾ cup (150g) granulated sugar
2 large eggs, at room temperature
1½ teaspoons vanilla extract
½ cup (120g) sour cream, at room temperature
½ cup (125ml) whole milk, at room temperature
2¼ cups (280g) all-purpose flour
2 teaspoons baking powder
½ teaspoon baking soda
⅛ teaspoon ground nutmeg
¾ teaspoon salt
2 cups (240g) powdered sugar, for coating (optional)

1. Preheat the oven to 350°F. Spray your donut pans with nonstick cooking spray.
2. Place the melted butter, canola oil, granulated sugar, eggs, vanilla, sour cream, and milk in a large mixing bowl. Whisk until smooth.
3. Add the flour, baking powder, baking soda, nutmeg, and salt to the bowl. Continue whisking until the mixture is combined into a smooth batter.

4. Divide the batter evenly among the prepared cavities, filling them a touch over ¾ full. Transfer the pans to the middle rack of the oven.

5. Bake for 12 to 14 minutes for standard donuts, 7 to 8 minutes for mini donuts, or 14 to 16 minutes for donut holes. If using a donut maker, follow the manufacturer's instructions. The donuts are done when a toothpick inserted comes out clean.

6. Remove the pans from the oven and allow the donuts to cool for 10 minutes. Carefully remove the donuts from the pans, and transfer them to wire racks to cool completely, 15 to 20 minutes more.

7. For sugared donuts, place the powdered sugar in a large, shallow mixing bowl shortly before serving. Dredge each donut in the sugar, turning to coat both sides.

INGREDIENT TIP The small amount of nutmeg in the batter gives these donuts their authentic bakery taste!

VARIATION TIP For Cinnamon-Sugar Cake Donuts, stir 3 tablespoons of ground cinnamon into the powdered sugar before coating.

CHOCOLATE CAKE DONUTS

PREP TIME 10 MINUTES | **BAKE TIME** 20 MINUTES | **INACTIVE TIME** 30 MINUTES

I admit I'm a fairly picky person about a lot of things, but I'm especially picky about chocolate cake donuts! When done right, they're one of my favorites, but often they're dry and lack real chocolate flavor. As far as I'm concerned, a good chocolate donut should be decadent enough to make me question whether I'm having breakfast or dessert, without being too sweet. I bake these chocolate donuts all the time; whether left as is, rolled in powdered sugar, or glazed, they are always sure to please.

MAKES

15 DONUTS

75 MINI
DONUTS

45 DONUT
HOLES

DONUT MAKER

MAKE IT MINI

ONE BOWL

Nonstick cooking spray

6 tablespoons (84g)
unsalted butter, melted

2 tablespoons (30ml)
canola oil

½ cup (100g)
granulated sugar

¼ cup (50g) firmly packed
light brown sugar

2 large eggs, at
room temperature

1 teaspoon vanilla extract

½ cup (120g) sour cream,
at room temperature

½ cup (125ml) whole milk,
at room temperature

1½ cups (184g)
all-purpose flour

⅔ cup (64g) unsweetened
cocoa powder

1½ teaspoons baking powder

1 teaspoon baking soda

¾ teaspoon salt

2 cups (240g) powdered
sugar, for coating
(optional)

1. Preheat the oven to 350°F. Spray your donut pans with non-stick cooking spray.
2. Place the melted butter, canola oil, granulated sugar, brown sugar, eggs, vanilla, sour cream, and milk in a large mixing bowl. Whisk until smooth.

3. Add the flour, cocoa powder, baking powder, baking soda, and salt to the bowl. Continue whisking until the mixture is combined into a smooth batter.

4. Divide the batter evenly among the prepared cavities, filling them a touch over ¾ full. Transfer the pans to the middle rack of the oven.

5. Bake for 12 to 14 minutes for standard donuts, 7 to 8 minutes for mini donuts, or 14 to 16 minutes for donut holes. If using a donut maker, follow the manufacturer's instructions. The donuts are done when a toothpick inserted comes out clean.

6. Remove the pans from the oven and allow the donuts to cool for 10 minutes. Carefully remove the donuts from the pans, and transfer them to wire racks to cool completely, 15 to 20 minutes more.

7. For sugared donuts, place the powdered sugar in a large, shallow mixing bowl shortly before serving. Dredge each donut in the sugar, turning to coat both sides.

GLUTEN-FREE OLD-FASHIONED CAKE DONUTS

PREP TIME 15 MINUTES | **BAKE TIME** 20 MINUTES | **INACTIVE TIME** 35 MINUTES

Regardless of a person's dietary restrictions, they should be able to enjoy delicious treats without having to hunt for unusual or expensive ingredients, and these donuts are a cinch to make. I especially love them with a full coat of Basic Vanilla Glaze (page 60) or dipped in Basic Chocolate Icing (page 68) and topped with sprinkles, but all the glazes in this book are gluten-free!

MAKES

15 DONUTS

75 MINI DONUTS

45 DONUT HOLES

MAKE IT MINI

ONE BOWL

Nonstick cooking spray

6 tablespoons (84g) unsalted butter, melted

4 teaspoons (20ml) canola oil

¾ cup (150g) granulated sugar

2 large eggs, at room temperature

1½ teaspoons vanilla extract

½ cup (120g) sour cream, at room temperature

½ cup (125ml) whole milk, at room temperature

2¼ cups (310g) gluten-free all-purpose flour blend

2 teaspoons baking powder

½ teaspoon baking soda

⅛ teaspoon ground nutmeg

¾ teaspoon salt

2 cups (240g) powdered sugar, for coating (optional)

1. Preheat the oven to 350°F. Spray your donut pans with non-stick cooking spray.
2. Place the melted butter, canola oil, granulated sugar, eggs, vanilla, sour cream, and milk in a large mixing bowl. Whisk until smooth.
3. Add the flour, baking powder, baking soda, nutmeg, and salt to the bowl. Continue whisking until the mixture is combined into a smooth batter.

4. Divide the batter evenly among the prepared cavities, filling them a touch over ¾ full. Transfer the pans to the middle rack of the oven.

5. Bake for 12 to 14 minutes for standard donuts, 7 to 8 minutes for mini donuts, or 14 to 16 minutes for donut holes. The donuts are done when a toothpick inserted comes out clean.

6. Remove the pans from the oven and allow the donuts to cool for 15 minutes. Carefully remove the donuts from the pans, and transfer them to wire racks to cool completely, 15 to 20 minutes more.

7. For sugared donuts, place the powdered sugar in a large, shallow mixing bowl shortly before serving. Dredge each donut in the sugar, turning to coat both sides.

INGREDIENT TIP For the best donuts, look for cup-for-cup blends of gluten-free flour that list rice flour, tapioca starch, and/or potato starch as the main ingredients and have xantham gum, too. Avoid blends that start with garbanzo bean flour. Take note that while the volume measurement will be the same as wheat flour, gluten-free baking flour typically weighs around 20g heavier per cup.

TROUBLESHOOTING TIP Gluten-free donuts are a bit more tender than wheat flour donuts, so be sure they have cooled completely before removing them from the pan, as they'll be less prone to breaking.

‚UTEN-FREE CHOCOLATE CAKE DONUTS

PREP TIME 10 MINUTES | **BAKE TIME** 20 MINUTES | **INACTIVE TIME** 35 MINUTES

Sure, a square of pure chocolate is a welcome indulgence, but sometimes we all want a cakey, chocolatey baked good. With a light texture and plenty of cocoa, you'd never even know these donuts are gluten-free. Frosted with Basic Vanilla Icing (page 60) or Basic Chocolate Icing (page 68) and finished with colorful sprinkles, they're great to bring to bake sales or potlucks for everyone to enjoy.

MAKES

15 DONUTS

75 MINI DONUTS

45 DONUT HOLES

MAKE IT MINI

ONE-BOWL

Nonstick cooking spray

6 tablespoons (84g) unsalted butter, melted

2 tablespoons (30ml) canola oil

½ cup (100g) granulated sugar

¼ cup (50g) firmly packed light brown sugar

2 large eggs, at room temperature

1 teaspoon vanilla extract

½ cup (120g) sour cream, at room temperature

½ cup (125ml) whole milk, at room temperature

1½ cups (205g) gluten-free all-purpose flour blend

⅔ cup (64g) unsweetened cocoa powder

1½ teaspoons baking powder

1 teaspoon baking soda

¾ teaspoon salt

2 cups (240g) powdered sugar, for coating (optional)

1. Preheat the oven to 350°F. Spray your donut pans with nonstick cooking spray.
2. Place the melted butter, canola oil, granulated sugar, brown sugar, eggs, vanilla, sour cream, and milk in a large mixing bowl. Whisk until smooth.

3. Add the gluten-free flour, cocoa powder, baking powder, baking soda, and salt to the bowl. Continue whisking until the mixture is combined into a smooth batter.
4. Divide the batter evenly among the prepared cavities, filling them a touch over ¾ full. Transfer the pans to the middle rack of the oven.
5. Bake for 12 to 14 minutes for standard donuts, 7 to 8 minutes for mini donuts, or 14 to 16 minutes for donut holes. The donuts are done when a toothpick inserted comes out clean.
6. Remove the pans from the oven and allow the donuts to cool for 15 minutes. Carefully remove the donuts from the pans, and transfer them to wire racks to cool completely, 15 to 20 minutes more.
7. For sugared donuts, place the powdered sugar in a large, shallow mixing bowl shortly before serving. Dredge each donut in the sugar, turning to coat both sides.

INGREDIENT TIP See the tip on page 19 for choosing gluten-free flours.

TROUBLESHOOTING TIP See the tip on page 19 for removing gluten-free donuts from pans.

VEGAN CAKE DONUTS

PREP TIME 10 MINUTES | **BAKE TIME** 20 MINUTES | **INACTIVE TIME** 30 MINUTES

I followed a strict vegan diet for four years in my teens, and it was during that time I really learned to bake. Determined to prove to people that vegan desserts could be just as enjoyable as anything made with dairy and eggs, I would come home from school each afternoon and make at least one new recipe from my collection of vegan cookbooks. Now, years later and no longer vegan, I still insist that vegan baked goods can and should be delicious. These donuts use familiar ingredients while being entirely free of dairy and eggs and are so good they're sure to convert any skeptics.

MAKES

15 DONUTS

75 MINI
DONUTS

•

45 DONUT
HOLES

DONUT MAKER

MAKE IT MINI

ONE BOWL

Nonstick cooking spray
1⅓ cups (312ml)
    nondairy milk
1 teaspoon apple
    cider vinegar
¾ cup (150g)
    granulated sugar
6 tablespoons (90ml)
    canola oil
1½ teaspoons vanilla extract

2¼ cups (280g)
    all-purpose flour
¼ cup (32g) cornstarch
1½ teaspoons baking powder
1 teaspoon baking soda
¾ teaspoon salt
⅛ teaspoon ground nutmeg
2 cups (240g) powdered
    sugar, for coating
    (optional)

1. Preheat the oven to 350°F. Spray your donut pans with nonstick cooking spray.
2. Place the nondairy milk and apple cider vinegar in a large mixing bowl and whisk to combine. Allow the mixture to sit for 5 minutes. It may appear slightly curdled. Add the sugar, canola oil, and vanilla to the milk mixture. Whisk until combined.
3. Add the flour, cornstarch, baking powder, baking soda, salt, and nutmeg to the bowl. Continue whisking until the mixture is combined into a smooth batter.

4. Divide the batter evenly among the prepared cavities, filling them a touch over ¾ full. Transfer the pans to the middle rack of the oven.

5. Bake for 12 to 14 minutes for standard donuts, 7 to 8 minutes for mini donuts, or 14 to 16 minutes for donut holes. If using a donut maker, follow the manufacturer's instructions. The donuts are done when a toothpick inserted comes out clean.

6. Remove the pans from the oven and allow the donuts to cool for 10 minutes. Carefully remove the donuts from the pans, and transfer them to wire racks to cool completely, 15 to 20 minutes more.

7. For sugared donuts, place the powdered sugar in a large, shallow mixing bowl shortly before serving. Dredge each donut in the sugar, turning to coat both sides.

INGREDIENT TIP Unsweetened almond and cashew milk are my favorite nondairy milks. Soy milk and coconut milk are fine alternatives. White wine vinegar or lemon juice can be used instead of apple cider vinegar.

VARIATION TIP These donuts are a great base for a variety of glazes in this book, such as the Basic Vanilla Glaze (page 60), Basic Chocolate Icing (page 68), and more. Simply use an equal amount of nondairy milk instead of cow's milk.

VEGAN CHOCOLATE CAKE DONUTS

PREP TIME 10 MINUTES | **BAKE TIME** 20 MINUTES | **INACTIVE TIME** 35 MINUTES

These soft, fudgy donuts may be entirely vegan, but they are virtually indistinguishable from traditional chocolate cake donuts. Even the most scrutinous taste testers won't be able to tell the difference. I especially like them topped with Basic Chocolate Icing (page 68); just be sure to swap out the whole milk for nondairy milk in that recipe to keep them vegan.

MAKES

15 DONUTS

75 MINI DONUTS

•

45 DONUT HOLES

DONUT MAKER

MAKE IT MINI

ONE BOWL

Nonstick cooking spray
1¼ cups (300ml) nondairy milk
1 teaspoon apple cider vinegar
¾ cup (150g) granulated sugar
6 tablespoons (90ml) canola oil
1½ teaspoons vanilla extract
1½ cups (184g) all-purpose flour

¾ cup (82g) unsweetened cocoa powder
¼ cup (32g) cornstarch
1½ teaspoons baking powder
¾ teaspoon baking soda
¾ teaspoon salt
2 cups (240g) powdered sugar, for coating (optional)

1. Preheat the oven to 350°F. Spray your donut pans with nonstick cooking spray.
2. Place the nondairy milk and vinegar in a large mixing bowl and whisk to combine. Allow the mixture to sit for 5 minutes. It may appear slightly curdled. Add the sugar, canola oil, and vanilla to the milk mixture. Whisk until combined.
3. Add the flour, cocoa powder, cornstarch, baking powder, baking soda, and salt to the bowl. Continue whisking until the mixture is combined into a smooth batter.

4. Divide the batter evenly among the prepared cavities, filling them a touch over ¾ full. Transfer the pans to the middle rack of the oven.

5. Bake for 12 to 14 minutes for standard donuts, 7 to 8 minutes for mini donuts, or 14 to 16 minutes for donut holes. If using a donut maker, follow the manufacturer's instructions. The donuts are done when a toothpick inserted comes out clean.

6. Remove the pans from the oven and allow the donuts to cool for 10 minutes. Carefully remove the donuts from the pans, and transfer them to wire racks to cool completely, 15 to 20 minutes more.

7. For sugared donuts, place the powdered sugar in a large, shallow mixing bowl shortly before serving. Dredge each donut in the sugar, turning to coat both sides.

INGREDIENT TIP Unsweetened almond and cashew milk are my favorite choices of nondairy milks. Soy milk and coconut milk are fine alternatives. White wine vinegar or lemon juice can be used instead of apple cider vinegar.

CAKE MIX DONUTS

PREP TIME 10 MINUTES | **BAKE TIME** 20 MINUTES | **INACTIVE TIME** 30 MINUTES

Easy baked donuts become even easier with boxed cake mix. With so many different flavors available these days, have fun trying different combinations to find your favorite. Powdered sugar or any of the icings or glazes in this book are great toppings, but store-bought frostings can make the process even quicker.

MAKES

12 DONUTS

60 MINI
DONUTS

36 DONUT
HOLES

DONUT MAKER

HOMEMADE
HEAD START

MAKE IT MINI

ONE BOWL

Nonstick cooking spray
1 (15.25-ounce) box cake
    mix, flavor of choice
6 tablespoons (84g)
    salted butter, melted
1 tablespoon (15ml) canola oil
2 large eggs, at
    room temperature
½ cup (125ml) whole milk,
    at room temperature

1. Preheat the oven to 350°F. Spray your donut pan with non-stick cooking spray.
2. Place the cake mix, melted butter, canola oil, eggs, and milk in a large mixing bowl. Whisk until smooth and combined.
3. Divide the batter evenly among the prepared cavities, filling them a touch over ¾ full. Transfer the pan to the middle rack of the oven.
4. Bake for 12 to 14 minutes for standard donuts, 7 to 8 minutes for mini donuts, or 14 to 16 minutes for donut holes. If using a donut maker, follow the manufacturer's instructions. The donuts are done when a toothpick inserted comes out clean.
5. Remove the pans from the oven and allow the donuts to cool for 10 minutes. Carefully remove the donuts from the pans, and transfer them to wire racks to cool completely before serving, 15 to 20 minutes more.

ALLERGEN TIP For a gluten-free version, use gluten-free cake mix. Unsweetened nondairy milk may be used instead of whole milk.

APPLE CIDER DONUTS

PREP TIME 40 MINUTES | **BAKE TIME** 20 MINUTES | **INACTIVE TIME** 45 MINUTES

Having lived next door to an apple orchard for most of my childhood, I've enjoyed my fair share of fresh cider donuts. There's nothing so quintessentially fall to me, and since moving away, I find myself pining for one of those warm, spiced donuts every September. These baked apple cider donuts rival many of the fried versions I've eaten thanks to a simple technique that intensifies their cider flavor. They're finished with a light coating of cinnamon sugar, and I feel a bit closer to home every time I make them.

MAKES

15 DONUTS

75 MINI DONUTS

45 DONUT HOLES

DONUT MAKER

MAKE IT MINI

FOR THE CIDER DONUTS

3 cups (750ml) apple cider

Nonstick cooking spray

6 tablespoons (84g) unsalted butter, melted

4 teaspoons (20ml) canola oil

6 tablespoons (75g) firmly packed light brown sugar

¼ cup (50g) granulated sugar

2 large eggs, at room temperature

1 teaspoon vanilla extract

2¼ cups (280g) all-purpose flour

2 teaspoons baking powder

½ teaspoon baking soda

½ teaspoon ground cinnamon

¼ teaspoon ground nutmeg

¾ teaspoon salt

FOR THE APPLE-SPICED SUGAR COATING

¼ cup (57g) unsalted butter

½ cup (100g) granulated sugar

2 teaspoons ground cinnamon

1 teaspoon apple pie spice

⅛ teaspoon salt

CONTINUED ➡

APPLE CIDER DONUTS *CONTINUED*

1. Pour the apple cider into a medium saucepan and set the pan over medium-high heat. Bring the cider to a boil. Once boiling, reduce the heat to medium-low so the cider gently simmers. Allow the cider to simmer until it has reduced to 1 cup. This may take anywhere from 12 to 20 minutes. Remove the pan from the heat and allow the cider to cool for 10 to 15 minutes before proceeding with the donut batter.
2. Preheat the oven to 350°F. Spray your donut pans with non-stick cooking spray.
3. Place the melted butter, canola oil, brown sugar, granulated sugar, eggs, vanilla, and reduced apple cider in a large mixing bowl. Whisk until smooth.
4. Add the flour, baking powder, baking soda, cinnamon, nutmeg, and salt to the bowl. Continue whisking until the mixture is combined into a smooth batter.
5. Divide the batter evenly among the prepared cavities, filling them a touch over ¾ full. Transfer the pans to the middle rack of the oven.
6. Bake for 12 to 14 minutes for standard donuts, 7 to 8 minutes for mini donuts, or 14 to 16 minutes for donut holes. If using a donut maker, follow the manufacturer's instructions. The donuts are done when a toothpick inserted comes out clean.
7. Remove the pans from the oven and allow the donuts to cool for 10 minutes. Carefully remove the donuts from the pans, and transfer them to wire racks to cool completely, 15 to 20 minutes more.
8. Place the butter in a microwave-safe bowl. Microwave on high for 25 to 30 seconds, or until fully melted. Stir together the granulated sugar, cinnamon, apple pie spice, and salt in a separate shallow bowl.

9. To coat the donuts, brush a donut lightly on both sides with the melted butter. Place the donut facedown in the spiced sugar, then flip to coat the opposite side. Gently shake off any excess sugar and transfer the donut to a tray. Repeat with the remaining donuts.

TROUBLESHOOTING TIP If the cider reduces a little too much and you're left with less than the 1 cup needed for this recipe, simply add enough fresh apple cider to the reduced liquid until it equals 1 cup.

INGREDIENT TIP If you don't have apple pie spice, use pumpkin pie spice or additional cinnamon.

PUMPKIN DONUTS

PREP TIME 20 MINUTES | **BAKE TIME** 20 MINUTES | **INACTIVE TIME** 30 MINUTES

On the many mornings my father would drive me to school as a kid, we would stop for two coffees and one breakfast item, which we'd split. Come August we'd start counting the days until the pumpkin donuts would appear on the shelves. Now as an adult I tend to think those glazed orange donuts are overly sweet and lack real pumpkin flavor, so I created this recipe to enjoy throughout the fall. These are perfectly spiced, with no shortage of pumpkin. I lose count of how many batches I make each season.

MAKES

12 DONUTS

60 MINI DONUTS

36 DONUT HOLES

DONUT MAKER

MAKE IT MINI

FOR THE PUMPKIN DONUTS

Nonstick cooking spray

¼ cup (57g) unsalted butter, melted

¼ cup (60ml) canola oil

½ cup (100g) firmly packed dark or light brown sugar

¼ cup (50g) granulated sugar

¾ cup (180g) pumpkin puree

2 large eggs, at room temperature

½ teaspoon vanilla extract

1⅓ cups (165g) all-purpose flour

1 teaspoon baking powder

½ teaspoon baking soda

2 teaspoons pumpkin pie spice

½ teaspoon salt

FOR THE PUMPKIN-SPICED SUGAR COATING

¼ cup (57g) unsalted butter

½ cup (100g) granulated sugar

1½ teaspoons pumpkin pie spice

1½ teaspoons ground cinnamon

⅛ teaspoon salt

1. Preheat the oven to 350°F. Spray your donut pans with non-stick cooking spray.
2. Place the melted butter, canola oil, brown sugar, granulated sugar, pumpkin puree, eggs, and vanilla in a large mixing bowl. Whisk until smooth.
3. Add the flour, baking powder, baking soda, pumpkin pie spice, and salt to the bowl. Continue whisking until the mixture is combined into a smooth batter.
4. Divide the batter evenly among the prepared cavities, filling them a touch over ¾ full. Transfer the pans to the middle rack of the oven.
5. Bake for 12 to 14 minutes for standard donuts, 7 to 8 minutes for mini donuts, or 14 to 16 minutes for donut holes. If using a donut maker, follow the manufacturer's instructions. The donuts are done when a toothpick inserted comes out clean.
6. Remove the pans from the oven and allow the donuts to cool for 10 minutes. Carefully remove the donuts from the pans, and transfer them to wire racks to cool completely, 15 to 20 minutes more.
7. While the donuts cool, make the coating. Place the butter in a microwave-safe bowl. Microwave on high for 25 to 30 seconds, or until fully melted. Stir together the granulated sugar, pumpkin pie spice, cinnamon, and salt in a separate shallow bowl.
8. To coat the donuts, brush a donut lightly on both sides with the melted butter. Place the donut facedown in the spiced sugar, then flip to coat the opposite side. Gently shake off any excess sugar and transfer the donut to a tray. Repeat with the remaining donuts.

VARIATION TIP For Glazed Pumpkin Donuts, coat with Basic Vanilla Glaze on page 60.

SNICKERDOODLE DONUTS

PREP TIME 20 MINUTES | **BAKE TIME** 20 MINUTES | **INACTIVE TIME** 30 MINUTES

Aside from apple pie, it's tough to think of a dessert more American than the snickerdoodle cookie. The soft, pillowy sugar cookies with a crunchy cinnamon-sugar exterior are a bake sale favorite across the country. Interestingly enough, it's actually believed that the snickerdoodle did not originate in America but rather was derived from a German recipe called *schnecke knödel,* or "snail dumplings"! Whatever the history, the flavors of a snickerdoodle make for irresistible donuts.

MAKES

15 DONUTS

75 MINI
DONUTS

●

45 DONUT
HOLES

DONUT MAKER

MAKE IT MINI

FOR THE CAKE DONUTS

Nonstick cooking spray

6 tablespoons (84g)
    unsalted butter, melted

4 teaspoons (20ml)
    canola oil

½ cup (100g) firmly packed
    light brown sugar

¼ cup (50g)
    granulated sugar

2 large eggs, at
    room temperature

1½ teaspoons vanilla extract

½ cup (120g) sour cream,
    at room temperature

½ cup (125ml) whole milk,
    at room temperature

2¼ cups (280g)
    all-purpose flour

2 teaspoons baking powder

½ teaspoon baking soda

¼ teaspoon ground
    cinnamon

⅛ teaspoon ground nutmeg

¾ teaspoon salt

FOR THE CINNAMON-SUGAR COATING

4 tablespoons (57g)
    unsalted butter

½ cup (100g)
    granulated sugar

1 tablespoon ground
    cinnamon

⅛ teaspoon salt

1. Preheat the oven to 350°F. Spray your donut pans with non-stick cooking spray.

2. Place the melted butter, canola oil, brown sugar, granulated sugar, eggs, vanilla, sour cream, and milk in a large mixing bowl. Whisk until smooth.

3. Add the flour, baking powder, baking soda, cinnamon, nutmeg, and salt to the bowl. Continue whisking until the mixture is combined into a smooth batter.

4. Divide the batter evenly among the prepared cavities, filling them a touch over ¾ full. Transfer the pans to the middle rack of the oven.

5. Bake for 12 to 14 minutes for standard donuts, 7 to 8 minutes for mini donuts, or 14 to 16 minutes for donut holes. If using a donut maker, follow the manufacturer's instructions. The donuts are done when a toothpick inserted comes out clean.

6. Remove the pans from the oven and allow the donuts to cool for 10 minutes. Carefully remove the donuts from the pans, and transfer them to wire racks to cool completely, 15 to 20 minutes more.

7. While the donuts cool, make the coating. Place the butter in a microwave-safe bowl. Microwave on high for 25 to 30 seconds, or until fully melted. Stir together the granulated sugar, cinnamon, and salt in a shallow bowl.

8. To coat the donuts, brush a donut lightly on both sides with the melted butter. Place the donut facedown in the spiced sugar, then flip to coat the opposite side. Gently shake off any excess sugar and transfer the donut to a tray. Repeat with the remaining donuts.

VARIATION TIP For Chai Spice Donuts, substitute the milk in the donut batter for ½ cup strongly brewed chai tea. Coat with Chai Spiced Sugar: ½ cup granulated sugar, 2 teaspoons ground cinnamon, ½ teaspoon ground cardamom, ¼ teaspoon ground ginger, ⅛ teaspoon ground nutmeg, ⅛ teaspoon ground cloves, and a dash of black pepper.

BANANA BREAD DONUTS

PREP TIME 15 MINUTES | **BAKE TIME** 20 MINUTES | **INACTIVE TIME** 30 MINUTES

I f you're looking for a way to use up overripe bananas that isn't the typical loaf of banana bread, look no further than these donuts. Simple to make, soft, light, and packed with banana flavor, they're a breakfast or snack-time treat both kids and adults love.

MAKES

12 DONUTS

60 MINI DONUTS

36 DONUT HOLES

DONUT MAKER

MAKE IT MINI

ONE BOWL

Nonstick cooking spray
2 very large or 3 small
   bananas, peeled (300g)
¼ cup (57g) unsalted
   butter, melted
2 tablespoons (30ml)
   canola oil
⅓ cup (66g) firmly packed
   light brown sugar
⅓ cup (66g)
   granulated sugar

2 large eggs, at room
   temperature
½ teaspoon vanilla extract
1½ cups (184g)
   all-purpose flour
1 teaspoon baking powder
½ teaspoon baking soda
½ teaspoon ground cinnamon
½ teaspoon salt
1 cup (120g) powdered sugar,
   for coating (optional)

1. Preheat the oven to 350°F. Spray your donut pans with non-stick cooking spray.
2. Place the bananas in a large mixing bowl and mash them thoroughly with a fork. Add the melted butter, canola oil, brown sugar, granulated sugar, eggs, and vanilla. Whisk until the mixture is thoroughly combined.
3. Add the flour, baking powder, baking soda, cinnamon, and salt to the bowl. Mix the dry and wet ingredients together with a rubber spatula until mostly smooth.
4. Divide the batter evenly among the prepared cavities, filling them a touch over ¾ full. Transfer the pans to the middle rack of the oven.

5. Bake for 12 to 14 minutes for standard donuts, 7 to 8 minutes for mini donuts, or 14 to 16 minutes for donut holes. If using a donut maker, follow the manufacturer's instructions. The donuts are done when a toothpick inserted comes out clean.

6. Remove the pans from the oven and allow the donuts to cool for 10 minutes in the pan. Carefully remove the donuts from the pans, and transfer them to wire racks to cool completely, 15 to 20 minutes more.

7. For sugared donuts, place the powdered sugar in a large, shallow mixing bowl shortly before serving. Dredge each donut in the sugar, turning to coat both sides.

VARIATION TIP For Banana-Nut Donuts or Banana–Chocolate Chip Donuts, fold ¼ cup of finely chopped walnuts or miniature chocolate chips into the batter along with the dry ingredients.

INGREDIENT TIP Extra ripe bananas with many brown spots are ideal for baking. Fully brown or black bananas are too ripe to use.

COFFEE CAKE DONUTS

PREP TIME 15 MINUTES | **BAKE TIME** 15 MINUTES | **INACTIVE TIME** 35 MINUTES

C offee cake has always been one of my very favorite treats. Top anything with cinnamon streusel, and I lose all self-control. With these vanilla-laced sour cream donuts, there's more of that warm, crunchy crumble in each bite. Even better, they bake and cool in less than a quarter of the time of a whole cake, which is ideal if you're like me and want your coffee cake sooner rather than later!

MAKES

16 DONUTS

FOR THE CINNAMON STREUSEL TOPPING

¾ cup (92g)
all-purpose flour

⅓ cup (66g) firmly packed
light or dark brown sugar

1 tablespoon (12g)
granulated sugar

2 teaspoons ground
cinnamon

¼ teaspoon salt

¼ cup (57g) unsalted
butter, melted

FOR THE SOUR CREAM CAKE DONUTS

Nonstick cooking spray

6 tablespoons (84g)
unsalted butter, melted

4 teaspoons (20ml)
canola oil

¾ cup (150g)
granulated sugar

2 large eggs, at
room temperature

1½ teaspoons vanilla extract

½ cup (120g) sour cream,
at room temperature

½ cup (125ml) buttermilk,
at room temperature

2¼ cups (280g)
all-purpose flour

2 teaspoons baking powder

½ teaspoon baking soda

¾ teaspoon salt

⅛ teaspoon ground nutmeg

2 tablespoons powdered
sugar, for dusting

TO MAKE THE CINNAMON STREUSEL TOPPING

Place the flour, brown sugar, granulated sugar, cinnamon, and salt in a large mixing bowl. Stir with a fork to combine. Drizzle the melted butter into the bowl, and mix with the fork until the mixture forms large crumbs. Refrigerate while you prepare the donut batter.

TO MAKE THE SOUR CREAM CAKE DONUTS

1. Preheat the oven to 350°F. Spray your donut pans with nonstick cooking spray.
2. Place the melted butter, canola oil, granulated sugar, eggs, vanilla, sour cream, and buttermilk in a large mixing bowl. Whisk until well combined. A few lumps of sour cream are okay.
3. Add the flour, baking powder, baking soda, salt, and nutmeg to the bowl. Whisk until the batter is smooth and combined. Divide the batter evenly among the prepared cavities, filling them about ¾ full.
4. Remove the streusel topping from the refrigerator. Sprinkle an even amount over each donut. Gently press down on the crumbs to adhere them to the batter. Transfer the pans to the middle rack of the oven.
5. Bake for 12 to 14 minutes. The donuts are done when a toothpick inserted comes out clean.
6. Remove the pans from the oven and allow the donuts to cool for 10 to 15 minutes. Carefully remove the donuts from the pans, and transfer them to wire racks to cool completely, 15 to 20 minutes more.
7. Shortly before serving, dust the powdered sugar over the donuts using a fine-mesh sieve.

PANETTONE DONUTS

PREP TIME 10 MINUTES | **BAKE TIME** 20 MINUTES | **INACTIVE TIME** 30 MINUTES

I studied opera in college, and one summer I flew to Italy to immerse myself in the language, perform with a professional choir, and visit every bakery I could. I befriended an older Bolognese bakery owner who gave me free cookies and told me I had to return during *Natale*, or Christmas, when the panettone would arrive. Scented with saffron, anise, and citrus, and studded with dried fruit and candied peel, panettone is a yeasted cake-like bread that takes many days to make. These easy donuts incorporate all the flavors of traditional panettone but are ready to eat in under an hour!

MAKES

15 DONUTS

75 MINI DONUTS

45 DONUT HOLES

DONUT MAKER

MAKE IT MINI

ONE BOWL

Nonstick cooking spray
6 tablespoons (84g)
    unsalted butter, melted
4 teaspoons (20ml)
    canola oil
¾ cup (150g)
    granulated sugar
2 large eggs, at
    room temperature
1 teaspoon vanilla extract
½ cup (120g) sour cream,
    at room temperature
½ cup (125ml) whole milk,
    at room temperature
2¼ cups (280g)
    all-purpose flour

2 teaspoons baking powder
½ teaspoon baking soda
¾ teaspoon salt
1 teaspoon lemon zest
1 teaspoon orange zest
½ teaspoon anise seeds,
    crushed (optional)
¼ teaspoon ground
    cinnamon
½ cup golden or
    regular raisins
½ cup finely chopped
    candied peel
¼ cup powdered sugar,
    for dusting

1. Preheat the oven to 350°F. Spray your donut pans with non-stick cooking spray.
2. Place the melted butter, canola oil, granulated sugar, eggs, vanilla, sour cream, and milk in a large mixing bowl. Whisk until smooth.
3. Add the flour, baking powder, baking soda, salt, lemon zest, orange zest, anise seeds (if using), and cinnamon to the bowl. Continue whisking until the mixture is combined into a smooth batter. Fold in the golden raisins and candied peel.
4. Divide the batter evenly among the prepared cavities, filling them a touch over ¾ full. Transfer the pans to the middle rack of the oven.
5. Bake for 12 to 14 minutes for standard donuts, 7 to 8 minutes for mini donuts, or 14 to 16 minutes for donut holes. If using a donut maker, follow the manufacturer's instructions. The donuts are done when a toothpick inserted comes out clean.
6. Remove the pans from the oven and allow the donuts to cool for 10 minutes. Carefully remove the donuts from the pans, and transfer them to wire racks to cool completely, 15 to 20 minutes more.
7. Shortly before serving, dust the powdered sugar over the donuts using a fine-mesh sieve.

INGREDIENT TIP Candied peel is citrus rind preserved in sugar. It's a main ingredient in panettone and common throughout Italy. In the United States, it tends to show up only around the holidays, so be sure to grab some when you see it. Alternatively, you can use an equal amount of finely chopped dried apricots.

CHAPTER

3

glazed

GLAZED BLUEBERRY CAKE DONUTS

PREP TIME 25 MINUTES | **BAKE TIME** 20 MINUTES | **INACTIVE TIME** 50 MINUTES

I didn't discover blueberry donuts until I was in my early twenties, but they're now one of my top choices. I love the subtle berry flavor and crackly sweet glaze in every bite. Plus, their blueish-purple hue is so pretty! I use two full cups of fresh blueberries to make these; while that's enough to create undeniable blueberry flavor, the addition of blueberry extract makes them look and taste like they came from a bakery. If fresh blueberries aren't available, you can use frozen. Just be sure to measure the berries while still frozen, then thaw them completely before blending.

MAKES

15 DONUTS

75 MINI DONUTS

45 DONUT HOLES

DONUT MAKER

MAKE IT MINI

Nonstick cooking spray

8 ounces fresh blueberries (2 cups)

6 tablespoons (84g) unsalted butter, melted

4 teaspoons (20ml) canola oil

¾ cup (150g) granulated sugar

2 large eggs, at room temperature

1 teaspoon vanilla extract

2 teaspoons blueberry extract or flavoring

6 tablespoons (90g) sour cream, at room temperature

2¼ cups (280g) all-purpose flour

1½ teaspoons baking powder

¾ teaspoon baking soda

¾ teaspoon salt

1 recipe Basic Vanilla Glaze (page 60)

1. Preheat the oven to 350°F. Spray your donut pans with nonstick cooking spray.
2. Place the blueberries in the bowl of a high-powered blender or food processor. Process on high until very smooth; this may take several minutes. Tap the bowl on the counter a few times to remove any air bubbles, then measure 10 tablespoons of the puree into a large mixing bowl.

3. Add the melted butter, canola oil, granulated sugar, eggs, vanilla, blueberry extract, and sour cream to the bowl of puree. Whisk until smooth.

4. Add the flour, baking powder, baking soda, and salt to the bowl. Continue whisking until the mixture is combined into a smooth batter.

5. Divide the batter evenly among the prepared cavities, filling them a touch over ¾ full. Transfer the pans to the middle rack of the oven.

6. Bake for 12 to 14 minutes for standard donuts, 7 to 8 minutes for mini donuts, or 14 to 16 minutes for donut holes. If using a donut maker, follow the manufacturer's instructions. The donuts are done when a toothpick inserted comes out clean.

7. Remove the pans from the oven and allow the donuts to cool for 10 minutes. Carefully remove the donuts from the pans, and transfer them to wire racks to cool completely, 15 to 20 minutes more.

8. While the donuts cool, prepare the Basic Vanilla Glaze. Dip the donuts in the glaze, flipping to fully coat both sides. Allow the excess to drip back into the bowl, then transfer the donuts to wire racks for about 20 minutes, or until the glaze has dried.

INGREDIENT TIP Blueberry flavoring for culinary use is easy to find in the baking supplies aisle of any craft store or online. If you're unable to find it, you can still make these donuts; just know the blueberry flavor will be quite faint and the color won't be as vibrant.

LEMON POPPYSEED DONUTS

PREP TIME 20 MINUTES | **BAKE TIME** 20 MINUTES | **INACTIVE TIME** 50 MINUTES

I never gave much thought to lemon poppyseed muffins until I learned they're a favorite for many. I've even seen them ranked as the most popular muffin flavor in America on more than one list! The bright citrus combined with the subtle nuttiness of poppyseeds might be even better in donut form, with a tangy lemon glaze that's so good, you'll find it hard to not lick the bowl.

MAKES

15 DONUTS

75 MINI DONUTS

45 DONUT HOLES

DONUT MAKER

MAKE IT MINI

FOR THE LEMON POPPYSEED DONUTS

Nonstick cooking spray

6 tablespoons (84g) unsalted butter, melted

4 teaspoons (20ml) canola oil

¾ cup (150g) granulated sugar

2 large eggs, at room temperature

1 teaspoon vanilla extract

½ cup (120g) sour cream, at room temperature

½ cup (125ml) whole milk, at room temperature

2¼ cups (280g) all-purpose flour

2 teaspoons baking powder

½ teaspoon baking soda

¾ teaspoon salt

1 tablespoon lemon zest (from 2 large lemons)

4 teaspoons poppyseeds

FOR THE LEMON GLAZE

1½ cups (180g) powdered sugar, sifted, plus more as needed

¼ teaspoon salt

1 teaspoon vanilla extract

Juice from 1 large lemon, plus more as needed

TO MAKE THE LEMON POPPYSEED DONUTS

1. Preheat the oven to 350°F. Spray your donut pans with nonstick cooking spray.

2. Place the melted butter, canola oil, granulated sugar, eggs, vanilla, sour cream, and milk in a large mixing bowl. Whisk until smooth.

3. Add the flour, baking powder, baking soda, salt, lemon zest, and poppyseeds to the bowl. Continue whisking until the mixture is combined into a smooth batter.

4. Divide the batter evenly among the prepared cavities, filling them a touch over ¾ full. Transfer the pans to the middle rack of the oven.

5. Bake for 12 to 14 minutes for standard donuts, 7 to 8 minutes for mini donuts, or 14 to 16 minutes for donut holes. If using a donut maker, follow the manufacturer's instructions. The donuts are done when a toothpick inserted comes out clean.

6. Remove the pans from the oven and allow the donuts to cool for 10 minutes. Carefully remove the donuts from the pans, and transfer them to wire racks to cool completely, 15 to 20 minutes more. While the donuts cool, prepare the glaze.

TO MAKE THE LEMON GLAZE

1. Place the powdered sugar and salt in a large bowl. Add the vanilla and lemon juice. Whisk until the glaze is completely smooth. It should drizzle slowly from the whisk. If it's too runny, add a few tablespoons of powdered sugar. If it's too thick, add lemon juice 1 teaspoon at a time until the desired consistency is reached.

2. Dip each donut facedown into the glaze. Allow the excess to drip off, then transfer each donut back to the wire racks, glazed-side up. Let the glaze set for about 20 minutes, or until it has dried.

VARIATION TIP For Orange Poppyseed Donuts, replace the lemon zest and lemon juice with the zest and juice of a fresh orange. You may not need all the juice from the orange. Start with 2 tablespoons and adjust as necessary to reach the desired consistency.

MATCHA GREEN TEA DONUTS

PREP TIME 20 MINUTES | **BAKE TIME** 20 MINUTES | **INACTIVE TIME** 50 MINUTES

Vibrant green matcha powder is made from specially grown and harvested green tea leaves, giving it a higher caffeine content than most other teas, and is typically found in small canisters sold alongside the bagged and loose-leaf teas in grocery and natural foods stores. Its strong flavor can be described as earthy and a touch bitter, but it pairs well with the sweetness of these donuts. Their deep green color is beautiful, and a garnish of slivered almonds makes them look even more elegant.

MAKES

15 DONUTS

75 MINI
DONUTS

45 DONUT
HOLES

DONUT MAKER

MAKE IT MINI

FOR THE MATCHA GREEN TEA CAKE DONUTS

Nonstick cooking spray

6 tablespoons (84g) unsalted butter, melted

4 teaspoons (20ml) canola oil

½ cup (100g) granulated sugar

¼ cup (50g) packed light brown sugar

2 large eggs, at room temperature

1 teaspoon vanilla extract

½ cup (120g) sour cream, at room temperature

½ cup (125ml) milk, at room temperature

2¼ cups (280g) all-purpose flour

5 teaspoons matcha green tea powder

2 teaspoons baking powder

½ teaspoon baking soda

¾ teaspoon salt

FOR THE MATCHA GREEN TEA GLAZE

1½ cups (180g) powdered sugar, sifted, plus more as needed

1½ teaspoons matcha green tea powder, plus more for dusting

¼ teaspoon salt

1 teaspoon vanilla extract

2 to 3 tablespoons (30 to 45ml) whole milk

¼ cup slivered almonds, for garnish (optional)

TO MAKE THE MATCHA GREEN TEA CAKE DONUTS

1. Preheat the oven to 350°F. Spray your donut pans with nonstick cooking spray.
2. Place the melted butter, canola oil, granulated sugar, brown sugar, eggs, vanilla, sour cream, and milk in a large mixing bowl. Whisk until smooth.
3. Add the flour, matcha powder, baking powder, baking soda, and salt to the bowl. Continue whisking until the mixture is combined into a smooth batter.
4. Divide the batter evenly among the prepared cavities, filling them a touch over ¾ full. Transfer the pans to the middle rack of the oven.
5. Bake for 12 to 14 minutes for standard donuts, 7 to 8 minutes for mini donuts, or 14 to 16 minutes for donut holes. If using a donut maker, follow the manufacturer's instructions. The donuts are done when a toothpick inserted comes out clean.
6. Remove the pans from the oven and allow the donuts to cool for 10 minutes. Carefully remove the donuts from the pans, and transfer them to wire racks to cool completely, 15 to 20 minutes more. While the donuts cool, prepare the glaze.

TO MAKE THE MATCHA GREEN TEA GLAZE

1. Place the powdered sugar, matcha powder, and salt in a large bowl. Add the vanilla and 2 tablespoons of milk. Whisk until the glaze is completely smooth. It should drizzle slowly from the whisk. If it's too runny, add a few tablespoons of powdered sugar. If it's too thick, add milk 1 teaspoon at a time until the desired consistency is reached.
2. Dip each donut facedown into the glaze. Allow the excess to drip off, then transfer each donut back to the wire racks, glazed-side up. Sprinkle a few slivered almonds (if using) or dust with more matcha powder immediately after glazing. Let the glaze set for about 20 minutes, or until it has dried.

RED VELVET CAKE DONUTS

PREP TIME 20 MINUTES | **BAKE TIME** 20 MINUTES | **INACTIVE TIME** 50 MINUTES

Not quite vanilla, not quite chocolate, it's hard to determine exactly what red velvet *is*. It should be deeply hued, with hints of cocoa and vanilla, and have plenty of moisture and tang from real buttermilk. These donuts meet all the criteria, then go a step further with a thin coating of buttermilk glaze. You could even top them with Cream Cheese Frosting (page 82) instead for a more traditional cakey bite.

MAKES

15 DONUTS

75 MINI
DONUTS

45 DONUT
HOLES

DONUT MAKER

MAKE IT MINI

FOR THE RED VELVET CAKE DONUTS

Nonstick cooking spray

6 tablespoons (84g)
    unsalted butter, melted

4 teaspoons (20ml)
    canola oil

½ cup (100g)
    granulated sugar

¼ cup (50g) firmly packed
    light brown sugar

2 large eggs, at
    room temperature

1 teaspoon vanilla extract

1 cup (250ml) buttermilk

2 tablespoons red
    food coloring

2 cups (250g)
    all-purpose flour

¼ cup (24g) unsweetened
    cocoa powder

1½ teaspoons baking powder

1 teaspoon baking soda

¾ teaspoon salt

FOR THE BUTTERMILK GLAZE

2 cups (240g) powdered
    sugar, sifted

¼ teaspoon salt

1½ teaspoons vanilla extract

5 to 6 tablespoons (75 to
    90ml) buttermilk

TO MAKE THE RED VELVET CAKE DONUTS

1. Preheat the oven to 350°F. Spray your donut pans with nonstick cooking spray.

2. Place the melted butter, canola oil, granulated sugar, brown sugar, eggs, vanilla, buttermilk, and food coloring in a large mixing bowl. Whisk until smooth.

3. Add the flour, cocoa powder, baking powder, baking soda, and salt to the bowl. Continue whisking until the mixture is combined into a smooth batter.

4. Divide the batter evenly among the prepared cavities, filling them a touch over ¾ full. Transfer the pans to the middle rack of the oven.

5. Bake for 12 to 14 minutes for standard donuts, 7 to 8 minutes for mini donuts, or 14 to 16 minutes for donut holes. If using a donut maker, follow the manufacturer's instructions. The donuts are done when a toothpick inserted comes out clean.

6. Remove the pans from the oven and allow the donuts to cool for 10 minutes. Carefully remove the donuts from the pans, and transfer them to wire racks to cool completely, 15 to 20 minutes more.

TO MAKE THE BUTTERMILK GLAZE

1. Place the powdered sugar and salt in a large bowl. Add the vanilla and 5 tablespoons of buttermilk. Whisk until the glaze is completely smooth. It should drizzle easily from the whisk. If it's too thick, add buttermilk 1 teaspoon at a time until the desired consistency is reached.

2. Dip the donuts in the glaze, flipping to fully coat both sides. Allow the excess to drip back into the bowl, then transfer the donuts to wire racks for about 20 minutes, or until the glaze has dried.

INGREDIENT TIP I prefer to use red gel food coloring, available in craft stores and online. Its color is much more intense than the tiny bottles of liquid food coloring sold in grocery stores.

SPICED MOCHA DONUTS WITH KAHLÚA GLAZE

PREP TIME 20 MINUTES | **BAKE TIME** 20 MINUTES | **INACTIVE TIME** 45 MINUTES

I n Mexico, *chocolate de mesa* is used to make a warming drink similar to hot chocolate. Cinnamon, nutmeg, and a dash of cayenne pepper bring subtle heat to these donuts inspired by that drink, and a half cup of strong coffee in the batter amplifies the flavors. If you'd prefer not to use Kahlúa in the glaze, use additional brewed coffee instead.

MAKES

15 DONUTS

75 MINI DONUTS

45 DONUT HOLES

ADULTS ONLY

DONUT MAKER

MAKE IT MINI

FOR THE SPICED MOCHA DONUTS

- Nonstick cooking spray
- 6 tablespoons (84g) unsalted butter, melted
- 2 tablespoons (30ml) canola oil
- ½ cup (100g) granulated sugar
- ¼ cup (50g) firmly packed light brown sugar
- 2 large eggs, at room temperature
- 1 teaspoon vanilla extract
- ½ cup (120g) sour cream, at room temperature
- ½ cup (125ml) strong brewed coffee, at room temperature
- 1½ cups (184g) all-purpose flour
- ⅔ cup (64g) unsweetened cocoa powder
- 1½ teaspoons baking powder
- 1 teaspoon baking soda
- 1¼ teaspoons ground cinnamon
- Dash of ground nutmeg
- Dash of cayenne pepper
- ¾ teaspoon salt

FOR THE COFFEE-KAHLÚA GLAZE

- 1½ cups (180g) powdered sugar, sifted, plus more as needed
- ¼ teaspoon salt
- 1 teaspoon vanilla extract
- 1½ tablespoons (22ml) strong brewed coffee, plus more as needed
- 1½ tablespoons (22ml) Kahlúa coffee liqueur, plus more as needed

TO MAKE THE SPICED MOCHA DONUTS

1. Preheat the oven to 350°F. Spray your donut pans with nonstick cooking spray.

2. Place the melted butter, canola oil, granulated sugar, brown sugar, eggs, vanilla, sour cream, and coffee in a large mixing bowl. Whisk until smooth.

3. Add the flour, cocoa powder, baking powder, baking soda, cinnamon, nutmeg, cayenne, and salt to the bowl. Continue whisking until the mixture is combined into a smooth batter.

4. Divide the batter evenly among the prepared cavities, filling them a touch over ¾ full. Transfer the pans to the middle rack of the oven.

5. Bake for 12 to 14 minutes for standard donuts, 7 to 8 minutes for mini donuts, or 14 to 16 minutes for donut holes. If using a donut maker, follow the manufacturer's instructions. The donuts are done when a toothpick inserted comes out clean.

6. Remove the pans from the oven and allow the donuts to cool for 10 minutes. Carefully remove the donuts from the pans, and transfer them to wire racks to cool completely, 15 to 20 minutes more. While the donuts cool, prepare the glaze.

TO MAKE THE COFFEE-KAHLÚA GLAZE

1. Place the powdered sugar and salt in a large bowl. Add the vanilla, coffee, and Kahlúa. Whisk until the glaze is completely smooth. It should drizzle slowly from the whisk. If it's too runny, add a few tablespoons of powdered sugar. If it's too thick, add 1 teaspoon of coffee at a time until the desired consistency is reached.

2. Dip each donut facedown into the glaze. Allow the excess to drip off, then transfer each donut back to the wire racks, glazed-side up. Let the glaze set for about 15 minutes, or until it has dried.

IRISH COFFEE DONUTS

PREP TIME 20 MINUTES | **BAKE TIME** 20 MINUTES | **INACTIVE TIME** 45 MINUTES

Whenever my mother and I went out to a nice dinner when I was growing up, she would order an Irish coffee as her dessert. She'd always let me eat the whipped cream off the top and would sometimes let me sneak a single sip. I love Irish coffees now that I'm an adult, and since I also love donuts, I had to combine the two! These cake donuts get a double punch of coffee flavor from both brewed coffee and instant espresso powder before being topped with a generous layer of whiskey glaze.

MAKES

15 DONUTS

75 MINI DONUTS

45 DONUT HOLES

ADULTS ONLY

DONUT MAKER

MAKE IT MINI

FOR THE COFFEE DONUTS

Nonstick cooking spray

6 tablespoons (84g) unsalted butter, melted

4 teaspoons (20ml) canola oil

½ cup (100g) granulated sugar

¼ cup (50g) packed light brown sugar

2 large eggs, at room temperature

1 teaspoon vanilla extract

½ cup (120g) sour cream, at room temperature

½ cup (125ml) strong brewed coffee

2¼ cups (280g) all-purpose flour

1 teaspoon instant espresso powder

2 teaspoons baking powder

½ teaspoon baking soda

¾ teaspoon salt

Dash of ground nutmeg

FOR THE IRISH WHISKEY GLAZE

1½ cups (180g) powdered sugar, sifted, plus more as needed

¼ teaspoon salt

1 teaspoon vanilla extract

1½ tablespoons (22ml) strong brewed coffee, plus more as needed

1½ tablespoons (22ml) Irish whiskey

TO MAKE THE COFFEE DONUTS

1. Preheat the oven to 350°F. Spray your donut pans with nonstick cooking spray.

2. Place the melted butter, canola oil, granulated sugar, brown sugar, eggs, vanilla, sour cream, and coffee in a large mixing bowl. Whisk until smooth.

3. Add the flour, espresso powder, baking powder, baking soda, salt, and nutmeg to the bowl. Continue whisking until the mixture is combined into a smooth batter.

4. Divide the batter evenly among the prepared cavities, filling them a touch over ¾ full. Transfer the pans to the middle rack of the oven.

5. Bake for 12 to 14 minutes for standard donuts, 7 to 8 minutes for mini donuts, or 14 to 16 minutes for donut holes. If using a donut maker, follow the manufacturer's instructions. The donuts are done when a toothpick inserted comes out clean.

6. Remove the pans from the oven and allow the donuts to cool for 10 minutes. Carefully remove the donuts from the pans, and transfer them to wire racks to cool completely, 15 to 20 minutes more. While the donuts cool, prepare the glaze.

TO MAKE THE IRISH WHISKEY GLAZE

1. Place the powdered sugar and salt in a large bowl. Add the vanilla, coffee, and Irish whiskey. Whisk until the glaze is completely smooth. It should drizzle slowly from the whisk. If it's too runny, add a few tablespoons of powdered sugar. If it's too thick, add coffee 1 teaspoon at a time until the desired consistency is reached.

2. Dip each donut facedown into the glaze. Allow the excess to drip off, then transfer each donut back to the wire racks, glazed-side up. Let the glaze set for about 15 minutes, or until it has dried.

RUM RAISIN DONUTS

PREP TIME 20 MINUTES | **BAKE TIME** 20 MINUTES | **INACTIVE TIME** 45 MINUTES

I once ordered a mojito and when the bartender served it to me he said, "This one is rummy-yum-yum," which is the perfect way to describe these rum raisin donuts. The subtly spiced brown-sugar cake donuts are studded with rum-soaked raisins and fully coated in buttery rum glaze.

MAKES

15 DONUTS

75 MINI
DONUTS

45 DONUT
HOLES

ADULTS ONLY

DONUT MAKER

MAKE IT MINI

FOR THE RUM RAISIN DONUTS

⅓ cup raisins

½ cup (125ml) spiced rum

Nonstick cooking spray

6 tablespoons (84g)
    unsalted butter, melted

4 teaspoons (20ml)
    canola oil

½ cup (100g) packed dark
    or light brown sugar

¼ cup (50g)
    granulated sugar

2 large eggs, at
    room temperature

1½ teaspoons vanilla extract

½ cup (120g) sour cream,
    at room temperature

½ cup (125ml) whole milk,
    at room temperature

2¼ cups (280g)
    all-purpose flour

½ teaspoon ground
    cinnamon

2 teaspoons baking powder

½ teaspoon baking soda

¾ teaspoon salt

FOR THE BUTTER-RUM GLAZE

2 cups (240g) powdered
    sugar, sifted

¼ teaspoon salt

1 teaspoon vanilla extract

2 tablespoons (28g)
    unsalted butter, melted

4 to 5 tablespoons
    (60 to 75ml) spiced rum

TO MAKE THE RUM RAISIN DONUTS

1. Place the raisins in a small bowl and pour the rum over them. Cover the bowl and allow the raisins to soak for at least 30 minutes, and up to overnight.
2. Preheat the oven to 350°F. Spray your donut pans with non-stick cooking spray.
3. Place the melted butter, canola oil, brown sugar, granulated sugar, eggs, vanilla, sour cream, and milk in a large mixing bowl. Whisk until smooth.
4. Add the flour, cinnamon, baking powder, baking soda, and salt to the bowl. Continue whisking until the mixture is combined into a smooth batter. Drain the rum from the raisins and fold them into the batter until evenly distributed.
5. Divide the batter evenly among the prepared cavities, filling them a touch over ¾ full. Transfer the pans to the middle rack of the oven.
6. Bake for 12 to 14 minutes for standard donuts, 7 to 8 minutes for mini donuts, or 14 to 16 minutes for donut holes. If using a donut maker, follow the manufacturer's instructions. The donuts are done when a toothpick inserted comes out clean.
7. Remove the pans from the oven and allow the donuts to cool for 10 minutes. Carefully remove the donuts from the pans, and transfer them to wire racks to cool completely, 15 to 20 minutes more. While the donuts cool, prepare the glaze.

TO MAKE THE BUTTER-RUM GLAZE

1. Place the powdered sugar and salt in a large bowl. Add the vanilla, melted butter, and 4 tablespoons of spiced rum. Whisk until the glaze is completely smooth. It should drizzle easily from the whisk. If it's too thick, add rum 1 teaspoon at a time until the desired consistency is reached.
2. Dip the donuts in the glaze, fully coating both sides. Allow the excess to drip back into the bowl, then transfer the donuts to wire racks for about 15 minutes, or until the glaze has dried.

GINGERBREAD DONUTS

PREP TIME 20 MINUTES | **BAKE TIME** 20 MINUTES | **INACTIVE TIME** 45 MINUTES

Everyone has a favorite they reach for on a holiday cookie tray, and for me, it's gingerbread. I love the deep spices in the soft molasses cookies with slightly crisp edges. While these donuts may not have icing smiles on them, they are guaranteed to make *you* smile. With the perfect balance of wintery spices, they are an ideal holiday breakfast. I have three different glazes I like to use on these festive donuts: Basic Vanilla Glaze (page 60), Lemon Glaze (page 44), or when I'm feeling extra celebratory, the bourbon glaze included here.

MAKES

⬤
16 DONUTS

⬤
80 MINI DONUTS

●
48 DONUT HOLES

ADULTS ONLY

DONUT MAKER

MAKE IT MINI

FOR THE GINGERBREAD DONUTS

Nonstick cooking spray

¼ cup (57g) unsalted butter, melted

2 tablespoons (30ml) canola oil

½ cup (100g) firmly packed dark brown sugar

½ cup (150g) molasses

2 large eggs, at room temperature

1 teaspoon vanilla extract

½ cup (120g) sour cream, at room temperature

½ cup (125ml) whole milk, at room temperature

2½ cups (310g) all-purpose flour

1 tablespoon ground ginger

1 tablespoon ground cinnamon

¼ teaspoon ground nutmeg

¼ teaspoon ground cloves

2 teaspoons baking powder

¾ teaspoon baking soda

¾ teaspoon salt

FOR THE BOURBON GLAZE

2 cups (240g) powdered sugar

¼ teaspoon salt

1 teaspoon vanilla extract

3 to 4 tablespoons (45 to 60ml) whole milk

2 tablespoons (30ml) bourbon

TO MAKE THE GINGERBREAD DONUTS

1. Preheat the oven to 350°F. Spray your donut pans with nonstick cooking spray.
2. Place the melted butter, canola oil, brown sugar, molasses, eggs, vanilla, sour cream, and milk in a large mixing bowl. Whisk until smooth.
3. Add the flour, ginger, cinnamon, nutmeg, cloves, baking powder, baking soda, and salt to the bowl. Continue whisking until the mixture is combined into a smooth batter.
4. Divide the batter evenly among the prepared cavities, filling them a touch over ¾ full. Transfer the pans to the middle rack of the oven.
5. Bake for 12 to 14 minutes for standard donuts, 7 to 8 minutes for mini donuts, or 14 to 16 minutes for donut holes. If using a donut maker, follow the manufacturer's instructions. The donuts are done when a toothpick inserted comes out clean.
6. Remove the pans from the oven and allow the donuts to cool for 10 minutes. Carefully remove the donuts from the pans, and transfer them to wire racks to cool completely, 15 to 20 minutes more. While the donuts cool, prepare your choice of glaze.

TO MAKE THE BOURBON GLAZE

1. Place the powdered sugar and salt in a large bowl. Add the vanilla, 3 tablespoons of milk, and bourbon. Whisk until the glaze is completely smooth. It should drizzle easily from the whisk. If it's too thick, add milk 1 teaspoon at a time until the desired consistency is reached.
2. Dip the donuts in the glaze, flipping to fully coat both sides. Allow the excess to drip back into the bowl, then transfer the donuts to wire racks for about 15 minutes, until the glaze has dried.

EGGNOG DONUTS

PREP TIME 20 MINUTES | **BAKE TIME** 20 MINUTES | **INACTIVE TIME** 45 MINUTES

I f there's a beverage more divisive than eggnog, I haven't heard of it. People seem to either love or hate the thick, creamy drink that graces the shelves of the dairy aisle every holiday season. Personally, I'm happy to drink a small glass of eggnog, but I'm even more fond of using it in baked goods! It adds incredible richness to cakes, muffins, and these donuts while imparting a flavor that's so characteristic of the holidays. A thin coating of eggnog glaze and a pinch of nutmeg add a sweet finishing touch.

MAKES

15 DONUTS

75 MINI
DONUTS

45 DONUT
HOLES

DONUT MAKER

MAKE IT MINI

FOR THE EGGNOG DONUTS

Nonstick cooking spray

6 tablespoons (84g)
    unsalted butter, melted

2 teaspoons (10ml) canola oil

¼ cup (50g)
    granulated sugar

2 large eggs, at
    room temperature

1 teaspoon vanilla extract

1 cup (250ml) eggnog, at
    room temperature

2¼ cups (280g)
    all-purpose flour

2 teaspoons baking powder

½ teaspoon baking soda

¾ teaspoon salt

½ teaspoon ground cinnamon

¼ teaspoon ground nutmeg

FOR THE EGGNOG GLAZE

1½ cups (180g) powdered
    sugar, sifted, plus
    more as needed

¼ teaspoon salt

1 teaspoon vanilla extract

2½ to 3 tablespoons
    (37 to 45ml) eggnog

1 tablespoon (15ml) bourbon,
    spiced rum, or whole milk

Ground nutmeg, for dusting

TO MAKE THE EGGNOG DONUTS

1. Preheat the oven to 350°F. Spray your donut pans with nonstick cooking spray.

2. Place the melted butter, canola oil, granulated sugar, eggs, vanilla, and eggnog in a large mixing bowl. Whisk until smooth.

3. Add the flour, baking powder, baking soda, salt, cinnamon, and nutmeg to the bowl. Continue whisking until the mixture is combined into a smooth batter.

4. Divide the batter evenly among the prepared cavities, filling them a touch over ¾ full. Transfer the pans to the middle rack of the oven.

5. Bake for 12 to 14 minutes for standard donuts, 7 to 8 minutes for mini donuts, or 14 to 16 minutes for donut holes. If using a donut maker, follow the manufacturer's instructions. The donuts are done when a toothpick inserted comes out clean.

6. Remove the pans from the oven and allow the donuts to cool for 10 minutes. Carefully remove the donuts from the pans, and transfer them to wire racks to cool completely, 15 to 20 minutes more. While the donuts cool, prepare the glaze.

TO MAKE THE EGGNOG GLAZE

1. Place the powdered sugar and salt in a large bowl. Add the vanilla, 2½ tablespoons of eggnog, and bourbon. Whisk until the glaze is completely smooth. It should drizzle slowly from the whisk. If it's too runny, add a few tablespoons of powdered sugar. If it's too thick, add eggnog 1 teaspoon at a time until the desired consistency is reached.

2. Dip each donut facedown into the glaze. Allow the excess to drip off, then transfer each donut back to the wire racks, glazed-side up. Let the glaze set for about 15 minutes, or until it has dried. Place a small spoonful of nutmeg in a fine-mesh sieve and sprinkle a very light dusting over the tops of the donuts before serving.

INGREDIENT TIP Either full-fat or light eggnog may be used for this recipe.

CLASSIC RAISED DONUTS

PREP TIME 25 MINUTES | **BAKE TIME** 20 MINUTES | **INACTIVE TIME** 3 HOURS

Glazed rings, iced bars, filled shells, and sugared twists—raised donuts are a cornerstone of morning treats, serving as a blank canvas for an endless variety of frostings and fillings. Though it does require patience to allow the dough to rise, making it is quite easy, especially if you let a stand mixer do the work for you. (And if you don't have a stand mixer, see the Technique Tip.) The result is a light, fluffy donut with a touch of sweetness and no messy frying oil. And don't skip the glaze! The extra crackly layer of sweetness brings these donuts to a new level.

MAKES

ABOUT
12 DONUTS

FOR THE CLASSIC RAISED DONUTS

1 recipe Yeast Donut dough (page 100) prepared through step 6

Nonstick cooking spray
2 tablespoons (30ml) canola oil

FOR THE BASIC VANILLA GLAZE

2 cups (240g) powdered sugar, sifted
¼ teaspoon salt

1½ teaspoons vanilla extract
5 to 6 tablespoons (75 to 90ml) whole milk

TO FINISH THE YEAST DONUTS

1. Prepare the Yeast Donuts through step 6 as indicated on page 100.
2. Turn the dough onto the work surface. Use a rolling pin to very gently roll the dough to a ½-inch thickness. Use a donut cutter or 3½-inch and 1-inch circular cutters to stamp out as many donuts as you can, then carefully transfer them to the baking sheet. Gently collect the dough scraps and reroll, repeating the cutting process until you have used all the dough.

3. Spray the donuts with nonstick cooking spray and cover them loosely with plastic wrap or a clean kitchen towel. Allow the donuts to proof again for 30 to 45 minutes, or until they appear puffy. Preheat the oven to 350°F in the last 15 to 20 minutes of proofing.

4. Brush the donuts with the canola oil and transfer them to the upper-middle rack of the oven. Bake for 14 to 16 minutes, until the tops of the donuts are lightly golden and they sound slightly hollow when tapped. Remove the baking sheet from the oven and allow the donuts to cool for 15 to 20 minutes while you prepare the glaze.

TO MAKE THE BASIC VANILLA GLAZE

1. Place the powdered sugar and salt in a large bowl. Add the vanilla and 5 tablespoons of milk. Whisk until the glaze is completely smooth. It should drizzle easily from the whisk. If it's too thick, add milk 1 teaspoon at a time until the desired consistency is reached.

2. Dip the donuts in the glaze, flipping to fully coat both sides. Allow the excess to drip back into the bowl, then transfer the donuts to wire racks for about 20 minutes, or until the glaze has dried.

TECHNIQUE TIP You can make these by hand; just know the dough is sticky! Knead the donuts with firm pressure on a lightly floured surface, adding the softened butter by the spoonful as indicated in the instructions. The dough is ready when it's completely smooth and creates strands when gently pulled. If it rips apart, knead it longer. Too much flour on your work surface may change the consistency of the dough, so instead lightly dampen your hands or spray them with nonstick cooking spray to prevent sticking.

COCONUT DONUTS

PREP TIME 20 MINUTES | **BAKE TIME** 15 MINUTES | **INACTIVE TIME** 45 MINUTES

For those who love all things coconut, these triple-coconut donuts are as good as it gets. Coconut milk makes the cake donuts extra tender, which is the perfect textural contrast to the crunchy top layer of shredded coconut. A small amount of coconut extract in both the donuts and the glaze balances the flavors for a sweet, coconutty bite. I always associate coconut with springtime, and I love decorating these donuts to look like nests for Easter using colorful malted milk ball "eggs." The Variation Tip on page 64 details how to make them.

MAKES

15 DONUTS

75 MINI
DONUTS

DONUT MAKER

MAKE IT MINI

FOR THE COCONUT DONUTS

Nonstick cooking spray

6 tablespoons (84g)
   unsalted butter, melted

4 teaspoons (20ml)
   canola oil

½ cup (100g)
   granulated sugar

2 large eggs, at
   room temperature

1 teaspoon vanilla extract

1 teaspoon coconut extract

½ cup (120g) sour cream,
   at room temperature

½ cup (125ml) full-fat
   coconut milk

2¼ cups (280g)
   all-purpose flour

2 teaspoons baking powder

½ teaspoon baking soda

¾ teaspoon salt

Dash of ground nutmeg

FOR THE COCONUT GLAZE

1½ cups (180g) powdered
   sugar, sifted, plus
   more as needed

¼ teaspoon salt

1 teaspoon vanilla extract

1 teaspoon coconut extract

2½ to 4 tablespoons (36 to
   60ml) coconut milk

1½ cups shredded coconut,
   for topping

TO MAKE THE COCONUT DONUTS

1. Preheat the oven to 350°F. Spray your donut pans with non-stick cooking spray.
2. Place the melted butter, canola oil, granulated sugar, eggs, vanilla, coconut extract, sour cream, and coconut milk in a large mixing bowl. Whisk until smooth.
3. Add the flour, baking powder, baking soda, salt, and nutmeg to the bowl. Continue whisking until the mixture is combined into a smooth batter.
4. Divide the batter evenly among the prepared cavities, filling them a touch over ¾ full. Transfer the pans to the middle rack of the oven.
5. Bake for 12 to 14 minutes for standard donuts, or 7 to 8 minutes for mini donuts. If using a donut maker, follow the manufacturer's instructions. The donuts are done when a toothpick inserted comes out clean.
6. Remove the pans from the oven and allow the donuts to cool for 10 minutes. Carefully remove the donuts from the pans, and transfer them to wire racks to cool completely, 15 to 20 minutes more. While the donuts cool, prepare the glaze.

TO MAKE THE COCONUT GLAZE

1. Place the powdered sugar and salt in a large bowl. Add the vanilla, coconut extract, and 2½ tablespoons of coconut milk. Whisk until the glaze is completely smooth. It should drizzle slowly from the whisk. If it's too runny, add a few tablespoons of powdered sugar. If it's too thick, add coconut milk 1 teaspoon at a time until the desired consistency is reached.

CONTINUED ➡

COCONUT DONUTS *CONTINUED*

2. Place the shredded coconut in a shallow bowl. Dip a donut facedown into the glaze, allow the excess to drip off, and dip it immediately into the coconut, pressing down gently to adhere the shreds. Return the donut coconut-side up to the wire rack. Repeat with the remaining donuts. Let the coconut topping set for about 15 minutes before serving.

VARIATION TIP For Coconut Easter Nest Donuts, lay the shredded coconut in an even layer on a baking sheet. Toast in the oven at 300°F for 5 to 7 minutes, keeping a close eye on it, until very lightly browned. Remove the baking sheet from the oven and allow to cool completely before coating the donuts. Place three different colored malted milk ball "eggs" (or Jordan almonds) in the center of each donut.

INGREDIENT TIP I recommend using full-fat canned coconut milk, found on the shelves of the Asian foods aisle at the grocery store. Shake the can well before opening and using. Refrigerated coconut milk sold in cartons is a very different product that produces less optimal results.

CHAPTER

4

iced and frosted

ICED AND SPRINKLED CLASSICS

PREP TIME 20 MINUTES | **BAKE TIME** 15 MINUTES | **INACTIVE TIME** 30 MINUTES

Iconic frosted donuts with colorful sprinkles always manage to stand out in an assortment. Test your creative abilities with these hypercustomizable donuts. Add a couple of drops of red to the vanilla icing for a pretty pink, and top it with white sprinkles. Or opt for chocolate on chocolate, which will have you licking the bowl! If you're feeling adventurous, you can experiment with adding a teaspoon of a different flavoring extract like strawberry or almond. No matter what you do, you can't go wrong!

MAKES

12 TO
15 DONUTS

DONUT MAKER

1 recipe Classic Raised Donuts (page 60), Old-Fashioned Cake Donuts (page 14), or Chocolate Cake Donuts (page 16)

Assorted sprinkles, for topping (optional)

FOR THE BASIC VANILLA ICING

1½ cups (180g) powdered sugar, sifted

¼ teaspoon salt

1½ teaspoons vanilla extract

2 to 3 tablespoons (30 to 45ml) whole milk

Food coloring, for colored icing (optional)

FOR THE BASIC CHOCOLATE ICING

1½ cups (180g) powdered sugar, sifted

½ cup (45g) unsweetened cocoa powder

⅛ teaspoon salt

1 teaspoon vanilla extract

¼ cup (60ml) milk, plus more as needed

TO MAKE THE BASIC VANILLA ICING

Place the powdered sugar and salt in a large bowl. Add the vanilla and 2 tablespoons of milk. Whisk until the icing is completely smooth. It will be quite thick but should not be a paste. If it's too thick, add milk 1 teaspoon at a time until it is a consistency that can be spooned without resistance but isn't thin enough to drizzle off a whisk. For colored icing, add food coloring 1 drop at a time, stirring to combine, until your desired color is reached.

TO MAKE THE BASIC CHOCOLATE ICING

Place the powdered sugar, cocoa powder, and salt in a large bowl. Add the vanilla and milk. Whisk until the icing is completely smooth. It will be quite thick but should not be a paste. If it's too thick, add milk 1 teaspoon at a time until it is a consistency that can be spooned without resistance but isn't thin enough to drizzle off a whisk.

TO ASSEMBLE THE DONUTS

Dip a donut facedown into the icing. Gently lift it and use the back of a spoon to smooth the icing into an even layer. Return the donut to the wire rack, iced-side up. Scatter sprinkles (if using) over the icing. Repeat with the remaining donuts. Allow the icing to set for about 20 minutes, or until it has dried.

TECHNIQUE TIP To create Tie-Dye Donuts, place a few tablespoons of different-colored icings into a large mixing bowl. Use the tip of a knife to very gently swirl the colors together. Dip a donut facedown into the icing, then gently lift it straight up and place it on a wire rack. The icing should have a marbled effect. Repeat the process until the icing in the bowl is almost gone, then add new icing and swirl. Continue dipping, refilling, and swirling until all the donuts are iced. Allow the icing to set for about 20 minutes, or until it has dried.

NYC BLACK AND WHITE DONUTS

PREP TIME 25 MINUTES | **BAKE TIME** 15 MINUTES | **INACTIVE TIME** 50 MINUTES

I f you've ever stepped foot inside a New York City bakery, deli, or bodega, it's likely you've seen the striking black and white cookies. The big cake-like vanilla cookies have hints of citrus and are spread with a thick layer of hard icing, chocolate on one half and vanilla on the other. Like the cookies, these tangy vanilla cake donuts have a touch of citrus zest and are decorated beautifully with vanilla and chocolate icing, making for an eye-catching treat.

MAKES

15 DONUTS

75 MINI
DONUTS

DONUT MAKER

MAKE IT MINI

FOR THE NEW YORK–STYLE DONUTS

Nonstick cooking spray

6 tablespoons (84g)
   unsalted butter, melted

4 teaspoons (20ml)
   canola oil

¾ cup (150g)
   granulated sugar

2 large eggs, at
   room temperature

½ teaspoon vanilla extract

¾ teaspoon lemon zest

¾ teaspoon orange zest

½ cup (120g) sour cream,
   at room temperature

½ cup (125ml) buttermilk
   or whole milk, at
   room temperature

2¼ cups (280g)
   all-purpose flour

2 teaspoons baking powder

½ teaspoon baking soda

¾ teaspoon salt

FOR THE BLACK AND WHITE ICING

1½ cups (180g) powdered
   sugar, sifted

⅛ teaspoon salt

1 teaspoon vanilla extract

2½ to 4 tablespoons
   (36 to 60ml) milk

¼ cup (24g) unsweetened
   cocoa powder

TO MAKE THE NEW YORK–STYLE DONUTS

1. Preheat the oven to 350°F. Spray your donut pans with nonstick cooking spray.

2. Place the melted butter, canola oil, granulated sugar, eggs, vanilla, lemon zest, orange zest, sour cream, and buttermilk in a large mixing bowl. Whisk until smooth.

3. Add the flour, baking powder, baking soda, and salt to the bowl. Continue whisking until the mixture is combined into a smooth batter.

4. Divide the batter evenly among the prepared cavities, filling them a touch over ¾ full. Transfer the pans to the middle rack of the oven.

5. Bake for 12 to 14 minutes for standard donuts, or 7 to 8 minutes for mini donuts. If using a donut maker, follow the manufacturer's instructions. The donuts are done when a toothpick inserted comes out clean.

6. Remove the pans from the oven and allow the donuts to cool for 10 minutes. Set your wire cooling racks over a sheet of parchment paper. Carefully remove the donuts from the pans, and transfer them to the wire racks to cool completely, 15 to 20 minutes more. While the donuts cool, prepare the icing.

TO MAKE THE BLACK AND WHITE ICING

1. Place the powdered sugar and salt in a large bowl. Add the vanilla and 2½ tablespoons of milk. Whisk until the icing is completely smooth. It should be rather thick but still drizzle very slowly from a spoon. If it is too thick, add milk 1 teaspoon at a time until the desired consistency is reached.

2. Transfer half the icing to a separate bowl. Whisk in the cocoa powder until smooth. Add 1 teaspoon of milk if needed to make the "black" icing the same consistency as the white.

3. To frost the donuts, leave them arranged on the wire racks. Use a spoon to apply white icing to one half of each donut, letting any excess drip down through the racks. Once all the donuts are partially coated in white icing, repeat the process on the exposed halves using the chocolate icing. Let the icing set for about 20 minutes, or until it has dried.

MAPLE-ICED DONUTS

PREP TIME 25 MINUTES | **BAKE TIME** 15 MINUTES | **INACTIVE TIME** 3 HOURS

After moving to California from the Northeast, it became clear that donuts aren't the same on both coasts. West Coast donuts are over the top, with one exception: the maple bar. Golden yeast dough is topped with a thick layer of maple-flavored icing. Many bakeries add crispy bacon pieces, and the salty-sweet combo is mouthwatering, but you can omit them if you like.

MAKES

ABOUT
12 DONUTS

1 recipe Classic Raised
    Donuts (page 60), cut
    into rings or rounds

FOR THE MAPLE ICING
1½ cups (180g)
    powdered sugar
¼ teaspoon salt
1 tablespoon (15ml)
    real maple syrup

4 slices bacon, cooked,
    chopped, for topping
    (optional)

1½ teaspoons maple extract
1 teaspoon vanilla extract
1½ to 2 tablespoons
    (22 to 30ml) whole milk

1. Prepare the donuts and allow them to cool completely on wire racks.
2. To make the icing, place the powdered sugar and salt in a large bowl. Add the maple syrup, maple extract, vanilla, and 1½ tablespoons of milk. Whisk until the icing is completely smooth. It will be quite thick but should not be a paste. If it's too thick, add milk 1 teaspoon at a time until it is a consistency that can be spooned without resistance but isn't thin enough to drizzle off a whisk.
3. Dip a donut facedown into the icing. Gently lift it and use the back of a spoon to smooth the icing into an even layer. Return the donut to the wire rack, iced-side up. Sprinkle the bacon (if using) on top. Repeat with the remaining donuts. Allow the icing to set for about 20 minutes, or until dry.

COOKIES AND CREAM DONUTS

PREP TIME 20 MINUTES | **BAKE TIME** 15 MINUTES | **INACTIVE TIME** 50 MINUTES

The ever-popular ice cream flavor becomes a favorite donut in these vanilla cake donuts strewn with crushed cookie pieces, dipped in chocolate ganache icing, and topped with more cookie pieces. If you love the combination of crunchy chocolate wafers with sweet cream, these donuts are for you. Plus, they can easily be made vegan. What better way to start the day than with cookies as part of your breakfast? Because, as Cookie Monster would say, "Without me cookies, me just a monster."

MAKES

15 DONUTS

75 MINI
DONUTS

DONUT MAKER

MAKE IT MINI

FOR THE COOKIES AND CREAM DONUTS

Nonstick cooking spray

6 tablespoons (84g)
    unsalted butter, melted

4 teaspoons (20ml)
    canola oil

¾ cup (150g)
    granulated sugar

2 large eggs, at
    room temperature

1½ teaspoons vanilla extract

½ cup (120g) sour cream,
    at room temperature

½ cup (125ml) buttermilk
    or whole milk, at
    room temperature

2¼ cups (280g)
    all-purpose flour

2 teaspoons baking powder

½ teaspoon baking soda

¾ teaspoon salt

6 chocolate sandwich
    cookies, crushed

FOR THE CHOCOLATE GANACHE AND COOKIE TOPPING

4 ounces semisweet
    chocolate, finely chopped

1 tablespoon (14g)
    unsalted butter

⅓ cup (85ml) heavy cream

7 to 8 chocolate sandwich
    cookies, crushed,
    for topping

CONTINUED ➡

COOKIES AND CREAM DONUTS *CONTINUED*

TO MAKE THE COOKIES AND CREAM DONUTS

1. Preheat the oven to 350°F. Spray your donut pans with non-stick cooking spray.
2. Place the melted butter, canola oil, granulated sugar, eggs, vanilla, sour cream, and buttermilk in a large mixing bowl. Whisk until smooth.
3. Add the flour, baking powder, baking soda, and salt to the bowl. Continue whisking until the mixture is combined into a smooth batter. Fold in the crushed chocolate sandwich cookies.
4. Spoon the batter evenly among the prepared cavities, filling them a touch over ¾ full. Transfer the pans to the middle rack of the oven.
5. Bake for 12 to 14 minutes for standard donuts, or 7 to 8 minutes for mini donuts. If using a donut maker, follow the manufacturer's instructions. The donuts are done when a toothpick inserted comes out clean.
6. Remove the pans from the oven and allow the donuts to cool for 10 minutes. Carefully remove the donuts from the pans, and transfer them to wire racks to cool completely, 15 to 20 minutes more. While the donuts cool, prepare the ganache.

TO MAKE THE CHOCOLATE GANACHE

1. Place the chocolate and butter in a microwave-safe bowl. Microwave on high for 30 seconds, just until the chocolate appears slightly softened. Add the heavy cream to the bowl, and microwave for 20 to 30 seconds more, until the cream gently bubbles.
2. Remove the bowl from the microwave. Stir gently, until the chocolate is fully melted into the cream and the mixture is smooth and glossy. If any pieces of chocolate remain, microwave the bowl in additional 10-second increments, stirring after each time until the chocolate is fully melted and smooth.

3. Dip each donut facedown into the ganache. Allow the excess to drip off, then transfer each donut back to the wire racks, chocolate-side up. Sprinkle 1 generous teaspoon of crushed chocolate sandwich cookies over each donut immediately after dipping. Transfer the donuts to the refrigerator for about 20 minutes, or until the ganache is set.

VARIATION TIP For Double-Chocolate Cookies and Cream Donuts, fold 6 crushed sandwich cookies into the Chocolate Cake Donuts (page 16) batter. Or use peanut butter chocolate sandwich cookies and Peanut Butter Cup Donuts (page 78) for Peanut Butter Pie Donuts.

ALLERGEN TIP Most name-brand chocolate sandwich cookies are dairy-free! Make these donuts vegan by preparing the Vegan Cake Donuts (page 22) and folding 6 crushed cookies into the batter. For the ganache, use bittersweet chocolate (make sure there's no milk fat in the ingredients), omit the butter, and replace the heavy cream with an equal amount of full-fat coconut milk.

GRASSHOPPER PIE DONUTS

PREP TIME 20 MINUTES | **BAKE TIME** 15 MINUTES | **INACTIVE TIME** 50 MINUTES

T hese chocolate-mint cake donuts are topped with sweet mint icing and crushed chocolate cookies. Delicious any time of year, they're especially fun to make around St. Patrick's Day.

MAKES

15 DONUTS

75 MINI
DONUTS

DONUT MAKER

MAKE IT MINI

FOR THE CHOCOLATE-MINT DONUTS

Nonstick cooking spray

6 tablespoons (84g)
  unsalted butter, melted

2 tablespoons canola oil

½ cup (100g)
  granulated sugar

¼ cup (50g) firmly packed
  light brown sugar

2 large eggs, at
  room temperature

1 teaspoon vanilla extract

1 teaspoon peppermint extract

½ cup (120g) sour cream,
  at room temperature

½ cup (125ml) milk, at
  room temperature

1½ cups (184g)
  all-purpose flour

⅔ cup (64g) unsweetened
  cocoa powder

1½ teaspoons baking powder

1 teaspoon baking soda

¾ teaspoon salt

FOR THE MINT ICING AND COOKIE TOPPING

1½ cups (180g) powdered
  sugar, plus more
  as needed

¼ teaspoon salt

1 teaspoon vanilla extract

½ teaspoon
  peppermint extract

2 to 3 tablespoons (30 to
  45ml) whole milk

1 to 2 drops green food
  coloring (optional)

6 chocolate sandwich
  cookies, roughly
  crushed, for topping

TO MAKE THE CHOCOLATE-MINT DONUTS

1. Preheat the oven to 350°F. Spray your donut pans with nonstick cooking spray.

2. Place the melted butter, canola oil, granulated sugar, brown sugar, eggs, vanilla, peppermint extract, sour cream, and milk in a large mixing bowl. Whisk until well combined. A few lumps of sour cream are okay.

3. Add the flour, cocoa powder, baking powder, baking soda, and salt to the bowl. Whisk until the batter is smooth and combined.

4. Divide the batter evenly among the prepared cavities, filling them a touch over ¾ full. Transfer the pans to the middle rack of the oven.

5. Bake for 12 to 14 minutes for standard donuts, or 7 to 8 minutes for mini donuts. If using a donut maker, follow the manufacturer's instructions. The donuts are done when a toothpick inserted comes out clean.

6. Remove the pans from the oven and allow the donuts to cool for 10 minutes. Carefully remove the donuts from the pans, and transfer them to wire racks to cool completely, 15 to 20 minutes more.

TO MAKE THE MINT ICING

1. Place the powdered sugar and salt in a large bowl. Add the vanilla, peppermint extract, 2 tablespoons of milk, and food coloring (if using). Whisk until the icing is completely smooth. It should drizzle very slowly from the whisk. If it's too runny, add a few tablespoons of powdered sugar. If it's too thick, add milk 1 teaspoon at a time until the desired consistency is reached.

2. Once the donuts have cooled, carefully dip each one face-down into the icing. Allow any excess to drip off, then transfer them back to the wire racks, iced-side up. Sprinkle with crushed chocolate sandwich cookies immediately. Allow the topping to set for about 20 minutes before serving.

PEANUT BUTTER CUP DONUTS

PREP TIME 20 MINUTES | **BAKE TIME** 15 MINUTES | **INACTIVE TIME** 50 MINUTES

If I ask someone what their favorite candy is and they answer anything other than "peanut butter cups," I have a hard time understanding. In my mind, rich, salty peanut butter with creamy chocolate is a flavor combination rarely matched. I know I'm not alone in my adoration, as I see how people's faces light up anytime I bake something with chocolate and peanut butter. They say you can never please everyone, but I know from experience if you make these donuts, you can sure come close!

MAKES

15 DONUTS

75 MINI DONUTS

DONUT MAKER

MAKE IT MINI

FOR THE PEANUT BUTTER DONUTS

Nonstick cooking spray

6 tablespoons (84g) smooth peanut butter

¼ cup (57g) unsalted butter, melted

¼ cup (60ml) canola oil

½ cup (100g) firmly packed light brown sugar

6 tablespoons (75g) granulated sugar

2 large eggs, at room temperature

1 teaspoon vanilla extract

1 cup (250ml) buttermilk or whole milk, at room temperature

2¼ cups (280g) all-purpose flour

2 teaspoons baking powder

½ teaspoon baking soda

½ teaspoon salt

1 recipe Chocolate Ganache (page 73)

8 full-size peanut butter cups, finely chopped, for topping

1. Preheat the oven to 350°F. Spray your donut pans with nonstick cooking spray.
2. Place the peanut butter, melted butter, canola oil, brown sugar, granulated sugar, eggs, vanilla, and buttermilk in a large mixing bowl. Whisk until smooth.

3. Add the flour, baking powder, baking soda, and salt to the bowl. Continue whisking until the mixture is combined into a smooth batter.

4. Divide the batter evenly among the prepared cavities, filling them a touch over ¾ full. Transfer the pans to the middle rack of the oven.

5. Bake for 12 to 14 minutes for standard donuts, or 7 to 8 minutes for mini donuts. If using a donut maker, follow the manufacturer's instructions. The donuts are done when a toothpick inserted comes out clean.

6. Remove the pans from the oven and allow the donuts to cool for 10 minutes. Carefully remove the donuts from the pans, and transfer them to wire racks to cool completely, 15 to 20 minutes more.

7. While the donuts cool, prepare the ganache as indicated on page 73. Dip each donut facedown into the ganache. Allow the excess to drip off, then transfer each donut back to the wire racks, chocolate-side up. Sprinkle 1 generous teaspoon of finely chopped peanut butter cups over each donut immediately after dipping. Transfer the donuts to the refrigerator for about 20 minutes, or until the ganache is set.

INGREDIENT TIP Be sure to use a no-stir variety of peanut butter for these donuts. All-natural peanut butters with separation between the oil and nuts will not bake properly.

ALLERGEN TIP No-stir almond butter and store-bought almond butter cups can be used instead of peanut butter and peanut butter cups.

GERMAN CHOCOLATE CAKE DONUTS

PREP TIME 30 MINUTES | **BAKE TIME** 15 MINUTES | **INACTIVE TIME** 30 MINUTES

These decadent donuts are just like eating a slice of cake! The coffee, whether regular or decaf, will enhance their rich chocolate flavor, but you can substitute buttermilk or whole milk, if needed. Be sure to use unsweetened shredded coconut, as sweetened varieties are too sweet.

MAKES

15 DONUTS

75 MINI
DONUTS

DONUT MAKER

MAKE IT MINI

FOR THE COCONUT-PECAN TOPPING

½ cup (115g) unsalted butter

1 cup (100g) firmly packed
   light brown sugar

¾ cup plus 2 tablespoons
   (220ml) half and half

4 large egg yolks

1 teaspoon vanilla extract

¼ teaspoon salt

Dash of ground cinnamon

1 cup unsweetened
   shredded coconut

1 cup finely chopped pecans

FOR THE CHOCOLATE CAKE DONUTS

Nonstick cooking spray

6 tablespoons (84g)
   unsalted butter,
   melted

2 tablespoons (30ml)
   canola oil

½ cup (100g)
   granulated sugar

¼ cup (50g) firmly packed
   light brown sugar

2 large eggs, at
   room temperature

1 teaspoon vanilla extract

½ cup (120g) sour cream,
   at room temperature

½ cup (125ml) strong
   brewed coffee, at
   room temperature

1½ cups (184g)
   all-purpose flour

⅔ cup (64g) unsweetened
   cocoa powder

1½ teaspoons baking powder

1 teaspoon baking soda

¾ teaspoon salt

TO MAKE THE COCONUT-PECAN TOPPING

1. Place the butter in a medium saucepan and set it over medium heat. Heat until the butter is melted, then briefly remove the pan from the stove and whisk in the brown sugar, half and half, and egg yolks until thoroughly combined. Return the pan to the heat and bring the mixture to a low boil. Whisk steadily for about 5 minutes, or until the mixture has thickened enough to coat the back of a spoon.

2. Remove the pan from the heat. Stir in the vanilla, salt, cinnamon, coconut, and chopped pecans. Allow the topping to sit at room temperature while you prepare the donuts. It will thicken as it cools.

TO MAKE THE CHOCOLATE CAKE DONUTS

1. Preheat the oven to 350°F. Spray your donut pans with non-stick cooking spray.

2. Place the melted butter, canola oil, granulated sugar, brown sugar, eggs, vanilla, sour cream, and coffee in a large mixing bowl. Whisk until well combined. A few lumps of sour cream are okay.

3. Add the flour, cocoa powder, baking powder, baking soda, and salt to the bowl. Whisk until the batter is smooth and combined.

4. Divide the batter evenly among the prepared cavities, filling them a touch over ¾ full. Transfer the pans to the middle rack of the oven.

5. Bake for 12 to 14 minutes for standard donuts, or 7 to 8 minutes for mini donuts. If using a donut maker, follow the manufacturer's instructions. The donuts are done when a toothpick inserted comes out clean.

6. Remove the pans from the oven and allow the donuts to cool for 10 minutes. Carefully remove the donuts from the pans, and transfer them to wire racks to cool completely, 15 to 20 minutes more.

7. To finish the donuts, spoon the coconut pecan topping in a ring around the top of each donut, then use the back of the spoon to gently spread it into an even layer.

CARROT CAKE DONUTS

PREP TIME 30 MINUTES | **BAKE TIME** 15 MINUTES | **INACTIVE TIME** 50 MINUTES

I f I were ever stranded on a desert island and given the choice of one cake to bake in my beach oven for the rest of my life, it would be carrot cake. The spices and textures from the carrots, dried fruit, and nuts are irresistible to me, especially when topped with a generous layer of tangy cream cheese frosting.

MAKES

12 DONUTS

60 MINI
DONUTS

DONUT MAKER

MAKE IT MINI

FOR THE CARROT CAKE DONUTS

Nonstick cooking spray

½ cup canola oil

½ cup (100g) packed
    light brown sugar

⅓ cup (65g)
    granulated sugar

2 large eggs, at
    room temperature

¼ cup (80g) unsweetened
    applesauce

1 teaspoon vanilla extract

1½ cups (184g)
    all-purpose flour

1 teaspoon ground cinnamon

⅛ teaspoon ground nutmeg

⅛ teaspoon ground ginger

1 teaspoon baking powder

½ teaspoon baking soda

Scant ½ teaspoon salt

1⅓ cups (160g) finely
    grated carrots

⅓ cup raisins (optional)

FOR THE CREAM CHEESE FROSTING

8 ounces (225g) cream
    cheese, softened

⅓ cup (75g) unsalted
    butter, softened

1 teaspoon vanilla extract

1⅓ cups (160g)
    powdered sugar

Pinch of salt

¼ cup finely chopped
    walnuts, for topping
    (optional)

TO MAKE THE CARROT CAKE DONUTS

1. Preheat the oven to 350°F. Spray your donut pans with non-stick cooking spray.
2. Place the canola oil, brown sugar, granulated sugar, eggs, applesauce, and vanilla in a large mixing bowl. Whisk vigorously until smooth and combined.
3. Add the flour, cinnamon, nutmeg, ginger, baking powder, baking soda, and salt to the bowl. Continue whisking until the mixture is just combined. Fold in the grated carrots and the raisins (if using).
4. Spoon the batter evenly among the prepared cavities, filling them a touch over ¾ full. Transfer the pans to the middle rack of the oven.
5. Bake for 12 to 14 minutes for standard donuts, or 7 to 8 minutes for mini donuts. If using a donut maker, follow the manufacturer's instructions. The donuts are done when a toothpick inserted comes out clean.
6. Remove the pans from the oven and allow the donuts to cool for 10 minutes. Carefully remove the donuts from the pans, and transfer them to wire racks to cool completely, about 20 minutes more. Make the cream cheese frosting while the donuts cool.

TO MAKE THE CREAM CHEESE FROSTING

1. Place the cream cheese, butter, and vanilla in a large mixing bowl. Beat with a hand mixer on medium speed until smooth and creamy. Add the powdered sugar and salt. Beat on low speed until the sugar is incorporated, then increase the speed to medium-high and continue beating for 2 to 3 minutes more, or until the frosting is light and fluffy.
2. Spread the frosting around the top of each donut. Sprinkle with the walnuts (if using). Refrigerate the donuts for about 20 minutes before serving.

S'MORES DONUTS

PREP TIME 25 MINUTES | **BAKE TIME** 15 MINUTES | **INACTIVE TIME** 45 MINUTES

Whether it was toasting marshmallows over a bonfire at summer camp, by the fireplace on winter nights, or if you were like my family, on an electric stovetop, seemingly everyone has fond memories of making and eating s'mores. These graham cracker cake donuts with chocolate ganache icing and toasted marshmallows are an ode to the gooey treat. Serve them at a gathering and watch everyone's eyes light up brighter than a campfire!

MAKES

14 DONUTS

FOR THE GRAHAM CRACKER DONUTS

Nonstick cooking spray

6 tablespoons (84g) unsalted butter, melted

1 tablespoon canola oil

½ cup (100g) packed light brown sugar

3 tablespoons (37g) granulated sugar

2 large eggs, at room temperature

1 teaspoon vanilla extract

½ cup (120g) sour cream, at room temperature

½ cup (125ml) milk, at room temperature

1¾ cups (215g) all-purpose flour

¾ cup (75g) graham cracker crumbs

2 teaspoons baking powder

½ teaspoon baking soda

½ teaspoon salt

¼ teaspoon ground cinnamon

1 recipe Chocolate Ganache (page 73)

1 cup miniature marshmallows, for topping

1. Preheat the oven to 350°F. Spray your donut pans with non-stick cooking spray.
2. Place the melted butter, canola oil, brown sugar, granulated sugar, eggs, vanilla, sour cream, and milk in a large mixing bowl. Whisk until well combined. A few lumps of sour cream are okay.

3. Add the flour, graham cracker crumbs, baking powder, baking soda, salt, and cinnamon to the bowl. Whisk until the batter is smooth and combined.

4. Divide the batter evenly among the prepared cavities, filling them a touch over ¾ full. Transfer the pans to the middle rack of the oven.

5. Bake for 12 to 14 minutes. The donuts are done when a toothpick inserted comes out clean.

6. Remove the pans from the oven and allow the donuts to cool for 10 minutes. Carefully remove the donuts from the pans, and transfer them to wire racks to cool completely, 15 to 20 minutes more. While the donuts cool, prepare the ganache as indicated on page 73.

7. Dip each donut facedown into the ganache. Allow the excess to drip off, then transfer each donut onto a baking sheet, chocolate-side up. Adhere 6 or 7 miniature marshmallows to the top of each donut. Transfer the baking sheet to the freezer for 10 to 15 minutes to set the ganache.

8. Arrange an oven rack to sit 5 to 6 inches from the broiler and set the oven to broil. Remove the baking sheet of donuts from the freezer and transfer it to the top oven rack. Broil the marshmallows for 30 seconds to 1 minute, until they are puffy and deeply browned. Watch very closely to ensure they don't burn. Carefully remove the baking sheet from the oven and serve the donuts immediately.

VARIATION TIP To make Hot Chocolate Donuts, replace the graham cracker cake donuts with the Chocolate Cake Donuts (page 16) or Gluten-Free Chocolate Cake Donuts (page 20).

INGREDIENT TIP If boxed graham cracker crumbs aren't available, make your own. Use a food processor or blender to process about 5 full graham cracker sheets into fine crumbs.

CHOCOLATE STOUT DONUTS

PREP TIME 20 MINUTES | **BAKE TIME** 15 MINUTES | **INACTIVE TIME** 50 MINUTES

Even those who don't typically reach for stout are likely to enjoy these chocolatey, ganache-frosted cake donuts. Stout beer is added to both the batter and the ganache, which lends a subtle maltiness to each bite, and a sprinkle of crushed pretzels is the perfect finishing touch.

MAKES

15 DONUTS

75 MINI DONUTS

ADULTS ONLY

DONUT MAKER

MAKE IT MINI

FOR THE CHOCOLATE STOUT DONUTS

Nonstick cooking spray

6 tablespoons (84g) unsalted butter, melted

2 tablespoons (30ml) canola oil

¾ cup (150g) firmly packed light brown sugar

¼ cup (50g) granulated sugar

2 large eggs, at room temperature

1 teaspoon vanilla extract

½ cup (120g) sour cream, at room temperature

½ cup (125ml) stout, at room temperature

1½ cups (184g) all-purpose flour

⅔ cup (64g) unsweetened cocoa powder

1½ teaspoons baking powder

1 teaspoon baking soda

¾ teaspoon salt

FOR THE CHOCOLATE STOUT GANACHE

4 ounces semisweet chocolate, finely chopped

1 tablespoon (14g) unsalted butter

¼ cup (60ml) heavy cream

1½ tablespoons (22ml) stout

1 cup pretzels, roughly crushed, for topping

TO MAKE THE CHOCOLATE STOUT DONUTS

1. Preheat the oven to 350°F. Spray your donut pans with nonstick cooking spray.
2. Place the melted butter, canola oil, brown sugar, granulated sugar, eggs, vanilla, sour cream, and stout in a large mixing bowl. Whisk until well combined. A few lumps are okay.

3. Add the flour, cocoa powder, baking powder, baking soda, and salt to the bowl. Whisk until the batter is smooth and combined.

4. Divide the batter evenly among the prepared cavities, filling them a touch over ¾ full. Transfer the pans to the middle rack of the oven.

5. Bake for 12 to 14 minutes for standard donuts, or 7 to 8 minutes for mini donuts. If using a donut maker, follow the manufacturer's instructions. The donuts are done when a toothpick inserted comes out clean.

6. Remove the pans from the oven and allow the donuts to cool for 10 minutes. Carefully remove the donuts from the pans, and transfer them to wire racks to cool completely, 15 to 20 minutes more. While the donuts cool, prepare the ganache.

TO MAKE THE CHOCOLATE STOUT GANACHE

1. Place the chocolate and butter in a microwave-safe bowl. Microwave on high for 30 seconds, just until the chocolate appears slightly softened. Add the heavy cream and stout to the bowl, and microwave for 20 to 30 seconds more, until the cream gently bubbles. Remove the bowl from the microwave. Stir gently, until the chocolate is fully melted into the cream and the mixture is smooth and glossy. If any pieces of chocolate remain, microwave the bowl in additional 10-second increments, stirring after each time, until the chocolate is fully melted and smooth.

2. Dip each donut facedown into the ganache. Allow the excess to drip off, then transfer each donut back to the wire racks, chocolate-side up. Sprinkle 1 generous teaspoon of crushed pretzels over each donut immediately after dipping. Transfer the donuts to the refrigerator for about 20 minutes, or until the ganache is set.

SPIDERWEB DONUTS

PREP TIME 30 MINUTES | **BAKE TIME** 15 MINUTES | **INACTIVE TIME** 20 MINUTES

Halloween is my absolute favorite holiday. I love the costumes, the decorations, the movies, and of course the treats! I find myself plotting for October 31 at the beginning of August. These scary-yet-cute spiderweb donuts are my favorite kind of recipe: They seem intricate and impressive, but they're actually quick and easy to make. Both kids and adults will be creeping up to snag one before they're gone!

MAKES

15 DONUTS

1 recipe Chocolate Cake
    Donuts (page 16) or

FOR THE SPIDERWEB ICING
    1½ cups (180g) powdered
        sugar, sifted
    ¼ teaspoon salt
    1½ teaspoons vanilla extract
    2½ to 3 tablespoons (37 to
        45ml) whole milk
    Purple, orange, and/
        or neon green food
        coloring (optional)

Old-Fashioned Cake
    Donuts (page 14)

2 ounces bittersweet or
    semisweet chocolate,
    finely chopped
Assorted Halloween
    sprinkles or nonpareils
    (optional), for topping

Prepare your choice of donuts and allow them to cool completely on wire racks.

TO MAKE THE SPIDERWEB ICING

1. To make the icing, place the powdered sugar and salt in a large bowl. Add the vanilla, and 2½ tablespoons of milk. Whisk until the icing is completely smooth. It will be quite thick but should not be a paste. If it's too thick, add milk 1 teaspoon at a time until it is a consistency that can be spooned without resistance but isn't thin enough to drizzle

off a whisk. You can divide the white icing into bowls before adding a few drops of food coloring (if using) to make a variety of colors, or stick to a larger batch of one color.

2. Place the chocolate in a microwave-safe bowl and microwave on high in 30-second increments, stirring between each, until it is fully melted and smooth. Transfer the melted chocolate to a piping bag and snip a very small opening from the tip, about 2 millimeters.

3. To create the spiderwebs, dip a donut facedown into the icing. Allow the excess to drip off, then transfer the donut back to the wire rack, iced-side up. With a steady hand, pipe a circle of chocolate onto the icing around the donut's hole. Pipe two more circles spaced roughly 1 centimeter apart so there are 3 concentric circles on the icing. For the web effect, drag a toothpick or the tip of a sharp knife in a straight line through the 3 circles, starting from the hole and working outward. Repeat 5 more times around the donut, so the points of the web are at even diagonals. Scatter a few sprinkles over each donut (if using).

4. Repeat until all the donuts are a welcoming home for spiders. Once finished, allow the icing to set for about 20 minutes, or until it has dried.

HOLIDAY WREATH DONUTS

PREP TIME 30 MINUTES | **BAKE TIME** 15 MINUTES | **INACTIVE TIME** 20 MINUTES

Since donuts and wreaths are both ring shaped, it would be silly to not combine the two for an easy, festive treat! Give cake donuts a holiday makeover with decorated green buttercream frosting, an assortment of sprinkles, and adorable edible bows. While you can certainly spread the frosting over the donuts, I encourage you to try the decorative piping. It is truly simple to do and creates stunning wreaths that look almost too good to eat.

MAKES

15 DONUTS

HOMEMADE
HEAD START

1 recipe Old-Fashioned
Cake Donuts (page 14),
Chocolate Cake
Donuts (page 16),

or Cake Mix Donuts
(page 26)

FOR THE HOMEMADE VANILLA BUTTERCREAM

½ cup (115g) unsalted butter

1 ounce (28g) cream
cheese, softened

1½ teaspoons vanilla extract

2 cups (240g)
powdered sugar

¼ teaspoon salt

2 to 3 tablespoons (30 to
45ml) heavy cream

Blue and yellow (or green)
food colorings

FOR THE WREATHS

Assorted holiday colored
nonpareils or sprinkles

15 royal icing bows or
45 red M&M's

Prepare your choice of donuts and allow them to cool completely on wire racks.

TO MAKE THE HOMEMADE VANILLA BUTTERCREAM

1. To make the buttercream frosting, place the butter, cream cheese, and vanilla in a large mixing bowl. Beat with a hand mixer on medium speed until smooth and creamy. Add the powdered sugar, salt, and 2 tablespoons of heavy cream.

Beat on low speed until the sugar is incorporated, then add the food coloring. I prefer to mix a few drops each of blue and yellow, as I find it creates a more natural-looking green, but plain green food coloring is just fine to use. Increase the speed to medium-high and continue beating for 2 to 3 minutes more, or until the frosting is light and fluffy. If after a minute the frosting seems stiff, add 1 additional tablespoon of heavy cream.

2. To decorate the donuts, fit a pastry bag with a small open star tip (often labeled as tip #22) and fill the bag with the buttercream. Starting around the hole and working in circles, begin piping stars (see Technique Tip) around a donut, finishing a circle before moving outward to the next, until the entire top surface of the donut is covered. Alternatively, you can simply spread the frosting around the top of each donut (see Ingredient Tip).

3. Sprinkle the donuts with nonpareils and adorn each with a royal icing bow. If you can't find icing bows, three red M&M's arranged in an upside-down triangle look just as cute.

4. Refrigerate the donuts for about 20 minutes to allow the frosting to firm up before serving.

TECHNIQUE TIP To pipe a star, hold the piping bag perpendicular to the top of the donut and gently rest the tip on the surface. Squeeze the bag gently, pulling up about ¼ inch, then stop squeezing and lift away the bag to create a finished tip.

INGREDIENT TIP If you choose to spread the frosting instead of pipe it, store-bought vanilla frosting can be dyed green and used instead of homemade buttercream.

CHAPTER
5

filled

STRAWBERRY CHEESECAKE DONUTS

PREP TIME 30 MINUTES | **BAKE TIME** 15 MINUTES | **INACTIVE TIME** 3 HOURS

A slice of creamy, tangy cheesecake topped with fresh strawberries is a dessert hardly anyone can pass up! In these donuts, a whipped no-bake cheesecake cream swirled with strawberry jam fills soft yeasted pastry shells, which are then brushed with butter and coated in graham cracker crumbs. Now you can have your cake and eat your donut, too.

MAKES

ABOUT
12 DONUTS

1 recipe Yeast Donut
    dough (page 100)

¾ cup (220g) seedless
    strawberry jam

FOR THE WHIPPED CHEESECAKE FILLING

4 ounces (112g) cream
    cheese, softened

¼ cup (50g) granulated sugar

1 teaspoon vanilla extract

¾ cup (180ml) heavy
    cream, cold

FOR THE GRAHAM CRACKER COATING

1 cup (100g) graham
    cracker crumbs (about
    7 full sheets)

3 tablespoons (42g)
    unsalted butter, melted

Make the yeast donuts as indicated on page 100.

TO MAKE THE WHIPPED CHEESECAKE FILLING

1. Place the cream cheese, sugar, and vanilla in a medium mixing bowl. Use a hand mixer to beat on medium-high speed for 2 to 3 minutes, until the mixture is completely smooth. Add ¼ of the heavy cream to the bowl. Beat on low speed to incorporate the heavy cream into the cream cheese, then add the remaining cream. Turn the mixer to medium and beat for 2 to 3 minutes, just until the whipped cream holds stiff peaks. Don't overbeat.

2. Place the jam in a small bowl and stir it vigorously with a fork until fairly smooth.

3. Fit a pastry bag with a small round piping tip. Open the bag wide and spoon a few tablespoons of jam down one side of the bag, then spoon a few tablespoons of the cheesecake filling down the other so the two fillings are more or less side by side. Fill the bag only ¾ full.

4. Use a skewer to poke a hole through the side of a donut, stopping about ¾ deep. Insert the piping tip into the hole and squeeze the bag to fill the donut with the strawberry cheesecake filling. When the donut is full, you will feel a bit of resistance on the tip. Remove the bag and repeat with the remaining donuts, refilling the bag as needed. (To "fill" without a pastry bag, see the Technique Tip.)

TO MAKE THE GRAHAM CRACKER COATING

Place the graham cracker crumbs in a shallow bowl. Brush the donuts on all sides with the melted butter, then roll each through the graham cracker crumbs, flipping to liberally coat all sides. Refrigerate the donuts for 10 to 15 minutes before serving to set the crumbs and the filling.

TECHNIQUE TIP To skip the pastry bag: Cut the donuts in half lengthwise with a sharp knife (like a hamburger bun), spoon the fillings onto one half, and then sandwich the other half over it.

VARIATION TIP For an even quicker but slightly different strawberry cheesecake donut, substitute graham cracker cake donuts (page 84) for the yeast donuts and simply spoon the cheesecake filling and jam into the centers once cool. Forgo the graham cracker coating and instead dust the donuts with powdered sugar just before serving.

BOSTON CREAM DONUTS

PREP TIME 40 MINUTES | **BAKE TIME** 15 MINUTES | **INACTIVE TIME** 2½ HOURS

To me, Boston cream donuts are as much a hallmark of my childhood in New England as cider donuts, especially since I grew up in Massachusetts. While cider donuts are an essential part of fall, Boston cream is an all-occasion, anytime donut that was my absolute favorite as a little girl. Clearly, I've since expanded my love of donuts to include a *much* wider variety, but the classic Boston cream will always hold a special place in my heart and stomach.

MAKES

ABOUT
12 DONUTS

HOMEMADE
HEAD START

1 recipe Yeast Donut dough (page 100)

1 recipe Basic Chocolate Icing (page 68)

FOR THE VANILLA PASTRY CREAM FILLING

3 large egg yolks

½ cup (100g) granulated sugar

¼ cup (32g) cornstarch

2 cups (500ml) whole milk

2 teaspoons vanilla extract

¼ teaspoon salt

Make the yeast donuts as indicated on page 100. Cut the dough into 3.5-inch rounds; do not cut an inner hole. Prepare the pastry cream while the dough is proofing, as it needs time to chill.

TO MAKE THE VANILLA PASTRY CREAM FILLING

1. Place the egg yolks, granulated sugar, and cornstarch in the bottom of a medium saucepan. Whisk until completely smooth. Stream in the milk while whisking constantly, until the mixture is fully dissolved.
2. Set the pan over medium heat. Cook the cream, whisking steadily, until the mixture thickens and bubbles, 6 to 8 minutes. Once it's bubbling, remove the pan from the heat. Whisk in the vanilla and salt.

3. Transfer the pastry cream to a bowl and press a sheet of plastic wrap directly on the surface of the cream. Refrigerate for at least 2 hours, or until it is completely chilled.

TO ASSEMBLE THE DONUTS

1. Prepare the chocolate icing as indicated on page 68.
2. Fit a pastry bag with a small round piping tip and fill the bag ¾ full with pastry cream. Use a skewer to poke a hole through the side of a donut, stopping about ¾ deep. Insert the piping tip into the hole and squeeze the bag to fill the donut with cream. When the donut is full, you will feel a bit of resistance on the tip. Remove the bag and repeat with the remaining donuts, refilling the bag as needed. (To "fill" without a pastry bag, see the Technique Tip on page 95.)
3. Dip a donut facedown into the icing. Gently lift it and use the back of a spoon to smooth the icing into an even layer, if needed. Return the donut to the wire rack, iced-side up. Repeat with the remaining donuts. Allow the icing to set for about 20 minutes, or until it appears matte.

INGREDIENT TIP For a Homemade Head Start, use boxed instant vanilla pudding mix instead of homemade pastry cream. Whisk 1½ cups of cold whole milk into one 5.1-ounce packet of mix and refrigerate it for 20 minutes before filling the donuts.

CHOCOLATE CREAM–FILLED DONUTS

PREP TIME 30 MINUTES | **BAKE TIME** 15 MINUTES | **INACTIVE TIME** 3 HOURS

Though I have yet to visit France, I'm well aware that one of their most popular breakfast items is *pain au chocolat*. Directly translating to "chocolate bread," it's a sweet, flaky roll baked with a molten chocolate center. I like to think of these chocolate cream–filled donuts as the Americanized version of the French pastry. Airy yeast donuts are filled with an incredibly light whipped chocolate buttercream, then rolled in a pretty coating of powdered sugar. For an even easier version, use store-bought whipped chocolate frosting for the filling.

MAKES

ABOUT
12 DONUTS

HOMEMADE
HEAD START

1 recipe Yeast Donut
    dough (page 100)

FOR THE WHIPPED CHOCOLATE BUTTERCREAM FILLING

½ cup (114g) unsalted
    butter, softened
¼ teaspoon salt
1 teaspoon vanilla
    extract
1¾ cups (215g)
    powdered sugar

6 tablespoons (34g)
    unsweetened
    cocoa powder
6 tablespoons (90ml)
    heavy cream
1½ cups (180g) powdered
    sugar, for coating

Make the yeast donuts as indicated on page 100.

TO MAKE THE WHIPPED CHOCOLATE BUTTERCREAM FILLING

1. Place the butter, salt, and vanilla in a large mixing bowl. Beat with a hand mixer on medium speed until smooth and creamy. Add the powdered sugar, cocoa powder, and heavy cream. Beat on low speed until the ingredients are incorporated, then increase the speed to medium-high and continue beating for 3 to 4 minutes more, until the filling is very light and fluffy.

2. Fit a pastry bag with a small round piping tip and fill the bag ¾ full with the buttercream. Use a skewer to poke a hole through the side of a donut, stopping about ¾ deep. Insert the piping tip into the hole and squeeze the bag to fill the donut with buttercream. When the donut is full, you will feel a bit of resistance on the tip. Remove the bag and repeat with the remaining donuts, refilling the bag as needed. (To "fill" without a pastry bag, see the Technique Tip on page 95.)

3. Place the powdered sugar in a large, shallow bowl. Roll each donut through the sugar, flipping to liberally coat all sides.

VARIATION TIP For an easier but slightly different chocolate cream donut, substitute Old-Fashioned Cake Donuts (page 14) or Gluten-Free Old-Fashioned Cake Donuts (page 18). Coat the cooled donuts in powdered sugar, then pipe or spoon the chocolate buttercream into the centers.

SUGARED JELLY DONUTS

PREP TIME 25 MINUTES | **BAKE TIME** 20 MINUTES | **INACTIVE TIME** 3½ HOURS

Nothing compares to biting into one of these fluffy yeasted donuts bursting with sweet jam. I love seedless raspberry jam, but you can use whichever flavor you prefer. I do insist, however, that you be heavy-handed with the final coating of powdered sugar, as leaving a shameless trail of the sweet white dust in your wake is all part of the experience. A stand mixer will make these donuts even easier to bake, but if you don't have one, see the Technique Tip on page 61.

MAKES

ABOUT
12 DONUTS

FOR THE YEAST DONUTS

½ cup (125ml) water

½ cup (125ml) whole milk,
   plus more as needed

2 teaspoons (7g)
   active dry yeast

½ cup (100g) sugar

1 large egg

3½ cups (445g) all-purpose
   flour, plus extra for
   dusting work surface

¼ teaspoon baking soda

1 teaspoon salt

¼ cup (57g) unsalted
   butter, softened

Nonstick cooking spray

2 tablespoons (30ml)
   canola oil

1 cup seedless raspberry
   jam, for filling

4 tablespoons (57g)
   unsalted butter,
   for coating

1½ cups (100g) granulated
   sugar, for coating

⅛ teaspoon salt, for coating

TO MAKE THE YEAST DONUTS

1. Place the water and milk in a large measuring cup. Microwave for 20 to 30 seconds, or until very warm to the touch but not hot. Stir in the yeast.

2. Fit your stand mixer with a dough hook attachment. Pour the yeasted liquid into the stand mixer bowl. Add the sugar and egg. Stir to combine.

3. Add the flour, baking soda, and salt to the bowl. Turn the mixer to medium-low to combine the ingredients. Once the dough begins to come together, increase the mixer speed to medium. With the mixer running, begin adding the butter a spoonful at a time, waiting until each is mostly incorporated into the dough before adding the next.

4. Once all the butter is added, continue running the mixer until the dough is completely smooth and starts to collect around the dough hook, pulling away from the bottom and sides of the bowl. This may take up to 15 minutes. Scrape down the sides of the bowl with a rubber spatula as needed. The dough will be very tacky. If it appears very wet halfway into kneading, add 1 additional tablespoon of flour. If it appears a bit dry, add a few teaspoons of milk.

5. Spray a large mixing bowl with nonstick cooking spray. Transfer the dough to this bowl using a rubber spatula and clean, slightly dampened hands. Turn the dough to coat it lightly in the nonstick spray. Cover the bowl with a sheet of plastic wrap or a heavy, clean kitchen towel.

6. Place the bowl in a warm area and allow it to proof for 1½ to 2 hours, or until doubled in volume. When the dough is almost ready, line two large baking sheets with parchment paper. Dust a work surface liberally with flour.

7. Turn the dough onto the work surface. Use a rolling pin to very gently roll the dough to a ½-inch thickness. Use a 3-inch circular cutter to stamp out as many donuts as you can, and carefully transfer them to the baking sheets. Gently collect the dough scraps and reroll them, repeating the cutting process until you have used all the dough.

8. Spray the donuts with nonstick cooking spray and cover them loosely with plastic wrap or a clean kitchen towel.

CONTINUED ➡

Allow the donuts to proof again for 30 to 45 minutes, or until they appear puffy. Preheat the oven to 350°F during the last 15 to 20 minutes of proofing.

9. Brush the donuts with the canola oil and transfer them to the upper-middle rack of the oven. Bake for 14 to 16 minutes, until the tops of the donuts are lightly golden and they sound slightly hollow when tapped. Remove the baking sheets from the oven and allow the donuts to cool for about 20 minutes before filling and sugaring.

TO FILL AND SUGAR THE DONUTS

1. Place the jam in a small bowl and stir it vigorously with a fork until fairly smooth. Microwave the butter for 25 to 30 seconds, or until melted. Stir together the sugar and salt in a shallow bowl.

2. Fit a pastry bag with a small round piping tip and fill the bag ¾ full with jam. Use a skewer to poke a hole through the side of a donut, stopping about ¾ deep. Insert the piping tip into the hole and squeeze the bag to fill the donut with jam. When the donut is full, you will feel a bit of resistance on the tip. Remove the bag and repeat with the remaining donuts, refilling the bag as needed. (To "fill" without a pastry bag, see the Technique Tip on page 95.)

3. Brush a donut lightly on both sides with the butter, place it facedown in the sugar, and flip to coat both sides. Shake off any excess sugar and transfer to a tray. Repeat with the remaining donuts.

VARIATION TIP For PB&J Donuts, prepare the Peanut Butter Cream Filling on page 106. Reduce the jam to ½ cup. Fill a pastry bag ¾ full with alternating spoonfuls of the fillings. Fill the donuts as indicated above. Refill the bag as needed. For Dulce de Leche Donuts, use 1 cup of prepared dulce de leche for the jam.

APPLE PIE DONUTS

PREP TIME 40 MINUTES | **BAKE TIME** 20 MINUTES | **INACTIVE TIME** 3 HOURS

By far the most popular pie there is, what's not to love about crisp-tender apples piled high into a flaky, buttery crust? While some people savor every bite of the crust, my love for apple pie is all about the filling. These soft and doughy donuts rolled in powdered cinnamon sugar are the perfect vessel for sweet, spiced homemade apple filling, which is prepared on the stovetop and baked inside the donuts. For a Homemade Head Start, canned apple pie filling can be used instead. If you're feeling extra indulgent, break out the vanilla ice cream for apple pie donuts à la mode.

MAKES

12 DONUTS

HOMEMADE
HEAD START

1 recipe Yeast Donut dough
　　(page 100), prepared
　　though step 6

FOR THE APPLE PIE FILLING

2 medium Granny
　　Smith apples
2 tablespoons
　　(16g) cornstarch
¼ cup (50g)
　　granulated sugar
3 tablespoons (35g) firmly
　　packed light brown sugar

1 teaspoon ground cinnamon
⅛ teaspoon ground nutmeg
Dash of ground cloves
¼ teaspoon salt
1¼ cups (300ml) warm water
2 teaspoons (10ml) freshly
　　squeezed lemon juice

All-purpose flour, for dusting
　　the work surface
Nonstick cooking spray
2 tablespoons (30ml)
　　canola oil

1½ cups (180g) powdered
　　sugar, for coating
2 tablespoons ground
　　cinnamon, for coating
¼ teaspoon salt, for coating

CONTINUED ➡

APPLE PIE DONUTS *CONTINUED*

Prepare the Yeast Donuts through step 6 as indicated on page 100. While the donuts are proofing, prepare the apple filling.

TO MAKE THE APPLE PIE FILLING

1. Peel and core the apples. Finely dice them into ¼-inch pieces. Measure 2 cups of the diced apples and set aside. If there's extra, reserve for another use.
2. Whisk together the cornstarch, granulated sugar, brown sugar, cinnamon, nutmeg, cloves, and salt in a small saucepan. Add about ½ cup of warm water and whisk to dissolve the cornstarch. Pour in the remaining water and lemon juice and whisk to combine.
3. Set the saucepan over medium-high heat and bring to a boil. Once boiling, reduce the heat to medium-low so the liquid simmers. Carefully add the diced apples to the saucepan and stir to combine.
4. Let the apple mixture simmer for 6 to 9 minutes, stirring occasionally, until the apples are fork-tender. Remove the pan from the heat and allow the mixture to cool to room temperature, 30 to 40 minutes. You can speed the process by placing the saucepan in the refrigerator.

TO ASSEMBLE AND BAKE THE DONUTS

1. Once the dough has doubled in volume, turn it onto a generously floured work surface. Use a rolling pin to very gently roll the dough to a ½-inch thickness. Use a 3-inch circular cutter to stamp out your donuts. Gently collect the dough scraps and reroll them, repeating the cutting process until you have used all the dough.
2. Take a round of dough and gently roll it to be just under ¼-inch thick. Spoon about 1 tablespoon of apple filling into the center of the round, then collect the edges of the dough

to encompass the filling, pinching the dough together to fully seal the seams. Place the donut seam-side down onto a baking sheet. Repeat with the remaining dough and filling.

3. Spray the donuts with nonstick cooking spray and cover them loosely with plastic wrap or a clean kitchen towel. Allow the donuts to proof again for 30 to 45 minutes, or until they appear puffy. Preheat the oven to 350°F in the last 15 to 20 minutes of proofing.

4. Brush the donuts with the canola oil and transfer them to the upper-middle rack of the oven. Bake for 15 to 17 minutes, until the tops of the donuts are lightly golden and they sound slightly hollow when tapped. Remove the baking sheets from the oven and allow the donuts to cool for at least 20 minutes before sugaring.

5. Place the powdered sugar, cinnamon, and salt in a large, shallow bowl and whisk to combine. Roll each donut through the sugar, flipping to liberally coat all sides.

SCOTCHEROO DONUTS

PREP TIME 35 MINUTES | **BAKE TIME** 15 MINUTES | **INACTIVE TIME** 3 HOURS

I n the mid-1960s, Rice Krispies cereal printed a recipe on their boxes for "Scotcheroos." These were bars made from mixing cereal with peanut butter sugar syrup, pressing it into a pan, and pouring a blend of melted chocolate and butterscotch chips over the top. Peanut butter, chocolate, and butterscotch is a flavor combination that can do no wrong, and unsurprisingly makes for an amazingly delicious donut.

MAKES

ABOUT
12 DONUTS

1 recipe Yeast Donut dough (page 100)

¼ cup roasted salted peanuts, finely chopped, for topping

FOR THE PEANUT BUTTER CREAM FILLING

4 ounces (112g) cream cheese, softened

¼ cup (50g) granulated sugar

1 teaspoon vanilla extract

1 cup (250ml) heavy cream, cold

¼ cup (64g) smooth peanut butter

FOR THE CHOCOLATE-BUTTERSCOTCH GANACHE

2 ounces bittersweet chocolate, finely chopped

2 ounces butterscotch chips

1 tablespoon (14g) unsalted butter

⅓ cup (80ml) heavy cream

Make the Yeast Donuts as indicated on page 100. Cut the dough into 3.5-inch rounds; do not cut an inner hole.

TO MAKE THE PEANUT BUTTER CREAM FILLING

1. Place the cream cheese, sugar, and vanilla in a medium mixing bowl. Using a hand mixer, beat on medium-high speed for 2 to 3 minutes, until the mixture is completely smooth.

2. Add ¼ cup of the heavy cream to the bowl. Beat on low speed to incorporate it into the cream cheese mixture, then add the remaining cream. Beat on medium-high for 2 to 3 minutes, until the whipped cream holds soft peaks. Add the peanut butter and continue beating on medium-high speed for 1 to 2 minutes longer, just until the cream holds stiff peaks. Don't overbeat. Cover the bowl and refrigerate for at least 20 minutes, or until ready to use. While the cream chills, make the ganache.

TO MAKE THE CHOCOLATE-BUTTERSCOTCH GANACHE

Place the chocolate, butterscotch chips, and butter in a microwave-safe bowl. Microwave on high for 30 seconds, just until the chocolate appears slightly softened. Add the heavy cream to the bowl, and microwave for 20 to 30 seconds more, until the cream gently bubbles. Remove the bowl from the microwave. Stir gently, until the chocolate is fully melted into the cream and the mixture is smooth and glossy. If any pieces of chocolate remain, microwave the bowl in additional 10-second increments, stirring after each time until the chocolate is fully melted and smooth.

TO ASSEMBLE THE DONUTS

1. Fit a pastry bag with a small round piping tip and fill the bag ¾ full with peanut butter cream. Use a skewer to poke a hole through the side of a donut, stopping about ¾ deep. Insert the piping tip into the hole and squeeze the bag to fill the donut with cream. When the donut is full, you will feel a bit of resistance on the tip. Remove the bag and repeat with the remaining donuts, refilling the bag as needed. (To "fill" without a pastry bag, see the Technique Tip on page 95.)
2. Dip the donuts facedown into the ganache. Allow the excess to drip off, then transfer the donuts back to the wire racks, chocolate-side up. Sprinkle 1 scant teaspoon of chopped peanuts onto each donut. Refrigerate the donuts for at least 10 minutes, or until the ganache is set.

KEY LIME PIE DONUTS

PREP TIME 30 MINUTES | **BAKE TIME** 15 MINUTES | **INACTIVE TIME** 45 MINUTES

When it comes to dessert, I'll choose chocolate or spices over fruit or citrus every time, with one exception: key lime pie. If there's a slice on a menu, none of the other options matter. The tangy lime mixed with sweet cream and buttery, cinnamon-scented graham cracker crumbs is impossible to resist, whether in a pie or these unique donuts. Don't be intimidated by the various components—the cream filling is made while the donuts cool, and the glaze is prepared while the cream chills, so putting the three together is a breeze!

MAKES

14 DONUTS

1 recipe Graham Cracker
  Donuts (page 84)

FOR THE WHIPPED CHEESECAKE CREAM

4 ounces (112g)
  cream cheese, softened
¼ cup (50g)
  granulated sugar

1 teaspoon vanilla extract
1 cup (250ml) heavy
  cream, cold

FOR THE LIME GLAZE

1¼ cups (150g) powdered
  sugar, sifted, plus
  more as needed
¼ teaspoon salt
Zest of 1 lime

Juice of 1 lime, plus
  more as needed
¼ teaspoon vanilla extract
2 or 3 drops neon green
  food coloring (optional)

TO MAKE THE WHIPPED CHEESECAKE CREAM

1. Place the cream cheese, sugar, and vanilla in a medium mixing bowl. Use a hand mixer to beat on medium-high speed for 2 to 3 minutes, until the mixture is completely smooth.

2. Add ¼ cup of the heavy cream to the bowl. Beat on low speed to incorporate it into the cream cheese mixture, then add the

remaining cream. Turn the mixer to medium-high and beat for 2 to 3 minutes, just until the whipped cream holds stiff peaks. Don't overbeat. Cover the bowl and refrigerate for at least 20 minutes, or until ready to use. While the cream chills, make the glaze.

TO MAKE THE LIME GLAZE

Place the powdered sugar, salt, and lime zest in a large bowl. Add the lime juice, vanilla, and food coloring (if using). Whisk until the glaze is completely smooth. It should drizzle slowly from the whisk. If it's too runny, add a few tablespoons of powdered sugar. If it's too thick, add lime juice 1 teaspoon at a time until the desired consistency is reached.

TO ASSEMBLE THE DONUTS

1. Carefully remove the donuts from the pans and transfer them to a wire rack. Dip the donuts facedown into the glaze. Allow the excess to drip off, then transfer the donuts back to the wire racks, glazed-side up.

2. Once no more glaze drips from the donuts, transfer them to a parchment-lined baking sheet. Remove the whipped cheesecake cream from the refrigerator. Fit a pastry bag with a large open star tip and fill the bag ¾ full with the cream. Pipe the cream into the center of each donut, creating a 1-inch-high swirl on top of each hole. Alternatively, simply spoon a few tablespoons of the cream into the centers of the donuts. Transfer the donuts to the refrigerator to chill for 15 minutes before serving.

CANNOLI DONUTS

PREP TIME 30 MINUTES | **BAKE TIME** 15 MINUTES | **INACTIVE TIME** 50 MINUTES

Brown sugar ricotta donuts with notes of cinnamon and citrus, bittersweet chocolate ganache topping, rich ricotta whipped cream filling, and a garnish of pistachios and crunchy sugar cone pieces: Let's not even pretend these donuts are breakfast and respect them for what they are—a showstopping dessert. Though the recipe appears long, these donuts will look and taste like they took far more time than they do. In about an hour, you'll have created a stunning batch of donuts that will rival the pastry selection at any Italian bakery.

MAKES

15 DONUTS

FOR THE RICOTTA DONUTS

Nonstick cooking spray

6 tablespoons (84g)
   unsalted butter, melted

4 teaspoons (20ml)
   canola oil

¾ cup (150g) firmly packed
   light or dark brown sugar

2 large eggs, at
   room temperature

1 teaspoon vanilla extract

½ cup (125g) ricotta cheese,
   at room temperature

½ cup (125ml) milk, at
   room temperature

2¼ cups (280g)
   all-purpose flour

2 teaspoons baking powder

½ teaspoon baking soda

¾ teaspoon salt

½ teaspoon orange zest

½ teaspoon lemon zest

½ teaspoon ground cinnamon

FOR THE RICOTTA CREAM FILLING

4 ounces (112g)
   cream cheese, softened

4 ounces (112g)
   ricotta cheese

¼ cup (50g)
   granulated sugar

2 teaspoons vanilla extract

¼ teaspoon orange zest

¼ teaspoon lemon zest

⅛ teaspoon ground cinnamon

1 cup (250ml) heavy
   cream, cold

1 recipe Chocolate
    Ganache (page 73)
¼ cup shelled pistachios,
    finely chopped, for
    topping (optional)

2 sugar ice cream cones,
    finely crushed, for
    topping (optional)

TO MAKE THE RICOTTA DONUTS

1. Preheat the oven to 350°F. Spray your donut pans with non-stick cooking spray.
2. Place the melted butter, canola oil, brown sugar, eggs, vanilla, ricotta, and milk in a large mixing bowl. Whisk until well combined. A few lumps of ricotta are okay.
3. Add the flour, baking powder, baking soda, salt, orange zest, lemon zest, and cinnamon to the bowl. Whisk until the batter is smooth and combined.
4. Divide the batter evenly among the prepared cavities. Transfer the pans to the middle rack of the oven.
5. Bake for 12 to 14 minutes. The donuts are done when a toothpick inserted comes out clean.
6. Remove the pans from the oven and allow the donuts to cool for 10 minutes. Carefully remove the donuts from the pans and transfer them to wire racks to cool completely, 15 to 20 minutes more. While the donuts cool, prepare the ricotta cream filling.

TO MAKE THE RICOTTA CREAM FILLING

1. Place the cream cheese, ricotta, granulated sugar, vanilla, orange zest, lemon zest, and cinnamon in a medium mixing bowl. Use a hand mixer to beat on medium-high speed for 2 to 3 minutes, until the mixture is completely smooth.

CONTINUED ➠

2. Add ¼ cup of the heavy cream to the bowl. Beat on low speed to incorporate it into the ricotta mixture, then add the remaining cream. Turn the mixer to medium-high and beat for 2 to 3 minutes, just until the cream holds stiff peaks. Don't overbeat. Cover the bowl and refrigerate for at least 20 minutes, or until ready to use.

3. While the filling chills, make the ganache as indicated on page 73.

TO ASSEMBLE THE DONUTS

1. Carefully remove the donuts from the pans and transfer them to a wire rack. Dip each donut facedown into the ganache. Allow the excess to drip off, then transfer each donut to a parchment-lined baking sheet.

2. Remove the ricotta cream filling from the refrigerator. Fit a pastry bag with a large open star tip and fill the bag ¾ full with the filling. Pipe the filling into the center of each donut, creating a 1-inch-high swirl on top of each hole. Alternatively, simply spoon a few tablespoons of the filling into the centers of the donuts.

3. Sprinkle the chopped pistachios and crushed sugar cones over the donuts (if using). Transfer the donuts to the refrigerator for at least 20 minutes, or until the ganache is set.

CHAPTER

6

donut holes and donut desserts

BIRTHDAY CAKE DONUT HOLES

PREP TIME 15 MINUTES | **BAKE TIME** 20 MINUTES | **INACTIVE TIME** 50 MINUTES

To quote the famous Julia Child, "A party without cake is just a meeting." Have truer words ever been spoken? Though these colorful bites are donut holes, I promise they will readily turn any gathering into a celebration. Everyone loves this sweet and buttery take on the classic birthday cake, even when no one is turning another year older. These donut holes are a particularly fun contribution to bake sales or kids' events, but they're also appropriate to make on an average Tuesday as a reminder that life's a party.

MAKES

●

ABOUT
30 DONUT
HOLES

DONUT MAKER

HOMEMADE
HEAD START

FOR THE DONUT HOLES

Nonstick cooking spray

1 (15.25-ounce) box
confetti cake mix

6 tablespoons (84g)
salted butter, melted

1 tablespoon (15ml)
canola oil

2 large eggs, at
room temperature

½ cup (125ml) whole milk,
at room temperature

1 recipe Basic Vanilla
Glaze (page 60)

Rainbow nonpareils or
sprinkles, for topping

TO MAKE THE DONUT HOLES

1. Preheat the oven to 350°F. Spray two donut hole pans with nonstick cooking spray.
2. Place the cake mix, melted butter, canola oil, eggs, and milk in a large mixing bowl. Whisk until smooth and combined.
3. Divide the batter evenly among the prepared donut hole cavities, filling each almost to the top. Transfer the pans to the middle rack of the oven.

4. Bake for 15 to 17 minutes. If using a donut hole maker, follow the manufacturer's instructions. The donuts are done when a toothpick inserted comes out clean.
5. Remove the donut hole pans from the oven and allow the donut holes to cool for 10 minutes in the pan. Carefully remove the donut holes from the pan and transfer them to wire racks to cool completely, about 20 minutes.
6. While the donut holes cool, make the Basic Vanilla Glaze as indicated on page 60.
7. Submerge the donut holes in the glaze, allow the excess to drip back into the bowl, and transfer them to wire racks. Add a pinch of rainbow nonpareil or sprinkles to the top of each hole immediately after glazing. Let the donut holes sit for about 20 minutes, or until the glaze has dried.

VARIATION TIP If you'd rather forgo the boxed cake mix and make these donut holes from scratch, prepare the batter for Old-Fashioned Cake Donuts (page 14) and add ¼ cup rainbow sprinkles along with the dry ingredients.

CHOCOLATE-RASPBERRY DONUT HOLES

PREP TIME 20 MINUTES | **BAKE TIME** 20 MINUTES | **INACTIVE TIME** 30 MINUTES

My earliest memory of dessert is of a chocolate layer cake with raspberry sauce, made by my family's neighbor. I was only three years old when I first ate the decadent cake, but I was old enough to know I should request it for my fourth birthday party. And my fifth. These chocolate cake donut holes with raspberry jam filling are a bite-size homage to the cake that inspired my love of sweets.

MAKES

18 DONUT HOLES

DONUT MAKER

FOR THE CHOCOLATE CAKE DONUT HOLES

Nonstick cooking spray

3 tablespoons (42g) unsalted butter, melted

1 tablespoon (15ml) canola oil

¼ cup (50g) granulated sugar

2 tablespoons (25g) firmly packed light brown sugar

1 large egg, at room temperature

½ teaspoon vanilla extract

¼ cup (60g) sour cream, at room temperature

¼ cup (60ml) whole milk, at room temperature

¾ cup (92g) all-purpose flour

⅓ cup (32g) unsweetened cocoa powder

1 teaspoon baking powder

¼ teaspoon baking soda

½ teaspoon salt

⅓ cup (100g) seedless raspberry jam, for filling

1 cup (120g) powdered sugar, sifted, for topping

¼ cup (24g) unsweetened cocoa powder, sifted, for topping

TO MAKE THE CHOCOLATE CAKE DONUT HOLES

1. Preheat the oven to 350°F. Spray your donut hole pan with nonstick cooking spray.

2. Place the melted butter, canola oil, granulated sugar, brown sugar, egg, vanilla, sour cream, and milk in a large mixing bowl. Whisk until smooth.

3. Add the flour, cocoa powder, baking powder, baking soda, and salt to the bowl. Continue whisking until the mixture is combined into a smooth batter.

4. Divide the batter evenly among the prepared donut hole cavities, filling each almost to the top. Transfer the pan to the middle rack of the oven.

5. Bake for 15 to 17 minutes. If using a donut hole maker, follow the manufacturer's instructions. The donuts are done when a toothpick inserted comes out clean.

6. Remove the donut hole pans from the oven and allow the donut holes to cool for 10 minutes in the pan. Carefully remove the donut holes from the pan and transfer them to wire racks to cool completely, about 20 minutes.

TO FILL AND SUGAR THE DONUTS

1. Fit a pastry bag with a small round piping tip and fill the bag with the jam. Use a skewer to poke a hole into each donut hole, stopping about ⅔ deep. Insert the piping tip into the hole and squeeze the bag to fill the donut hole with jam. When the donut is full you will feel a bit of resistance on the tip. Be careful not to fill the hole so much that it splits open. Remove the bag and repeat with the remaining donut holes.

2. Whisk together the powdered sugar and cocoa powder in a medium bowl. Roll each donut hole through the sugar to fully coat.

VARIATION TIP For Chocolate-Caramel Donut Holes, substitute ⅓ cup of prepared salted caramel sauce for the raspberry jam.

FIRECRACKER DONUT HOLE POPS

PREP TIME 35 MINUTES | **BAKE TIME** 20 MINUTES | **INACTIVE TIME** 40 MINUTES

Red, white, and blue ice pops have been an American summertime standby for over 50 years. Originally called Bomb Pops, they adopted the name Firecracker in the late 1980s. These fun, patriotic donut pops are made by rolling donut holes in red, white, and blue decorating sugars, then arranging them on sticks to look like the popular frozen treat. But you don't have to wait until the Fourth of July to make them—the sugar colors can be customized for any celebration.

MAKES

●

12 DONUT HOLE POPS

DONUT MAKER

HOMEMADE HEAD START

FOR THE DONUT HOLES

Nonstick cooking spray

1 recipe Old-Fashioned Cake Donuts (page 14) or Cake Mix Donuts (page 26)

1 recipe Basic Vanilla Glaze (page 60)

½ cup white decorating sugar

½ cup blue decorating sugar

½ cup red decorating sugar

TO MAKE THE DONUT HOLES

1. Preheat the oven to 350°F. Spray two donut hole pans with nonstick cooking spray.
2. Prepare the batter for the donuts. Divide the batter evenly among the prepared donut hole cavities, filling each almost to the top. You should have at least 36 donut holes. Transfer the pans to the middle rack of the oven.
3. Bake for 15 to 17 minutes. If using a donut hole maker, follow the manufacturer's instructions. The donuts are done when a toothpick inserted comes out clean.

4. Remove the donut hole pans from the oven and allow the donut holes to cool for 10 minutes in the pan. Carefully remove the donut holes from the pan and transfer them to wire racks to cool completely, about 20 minutes.

5. While the donut holes bake and cool, place each color of decorating sugar in a separate bowl. Make the Basic Vanilla Glaze as indicated on page 60.

6. Submerge a donut hole in the glaze, allow the excess to drip back into the bowl, and immediately roll it through the white decorating sugar until it is entirely coated. Return the donut hole to the wire racks and repeat the process of glazing and coating in white sugar with 11 more donut holes. Next, glaze and coat 12 donut holes in blue decorating sugar, then glaze and coat the last 12 donut holes in red sugar.

7. Allow the donuts to sit on the wire racks for about 20 minutes, until the coating has dried.

TO ASSEMBLE THE POPS

To make the pops, gently poke a cake-pop stick through the center of a blue sugared donut hole, pushing the donut hole to sit about ¾ of the way down the stick. Follow with a white sugared donut hole, arranging it next to the blue. Place a red donut hole onto the stick, being sure the stick is inserted only about ¾ deep and does not poke through the top of the donut hole. Adjust the white and blue donut holes if needed so there are no gaps between the three donut holes. Set the donut hole pop on the wire racks and repeat until you have made all 12.

VARIATION TIP These pops are easily customizable. Use red, white, and green decorating sugar for Christmas; red, white, and pink for Valentine's Day; or orange, white, and yellow for Halloween.

EASY APPLE "FRITTERS"

PREP TIME 15 MINUTES | **BAKE TIME** 40 MINUTES | **INACTIVE TIME** 40 MINUTES

Golden brown, lightly spiced dough studded with crisp apples, and sized no smaller than a salad plate, apple fritters are an autumn delicacy. I used to wait until I found a stand selling them at the farmers' market to get my fix, but I recently discovered it is possible to bake these oversized pastries at home without compromising the characteristically crisp crust. The secret? An unexpected store-bought ingredient that makes these dangerously easy to make.

MAKES

6 LARGE
FRITTERS

HOMEMADE
HEAD START

FOR THE FRITTERS

1 (16.3oz) can
    refrigerated biscuits
1 small Granny Smith apple
2 tablespoons (25g) packed
    light brown sugar

1 recipe Basic Vanilla
    Glaze (page 60)

1 teaspoon ground cinnamon
¼ teaspoon pumpkin
    pie spice

1. Preheat the oven to 350°F. Line a baking sheet with parchment paper.
2. Remove the biscuit dough from the can and separate the precut pieces. Use a sharp knife to cut each biscuit into ¾-inch cubes, about 9 per piece. Place the biscuit dough in a large mixing bowl.
3. Peel and core the apple. Dice it into ¼-inch cubes and add to the bowl. Sprinkle brown sugar, cinnamon, and pumpkin

pie spice into the bowl and toss gently until the dough and apples are evenly coated.

4. With clean hands, divide the dough mixture into 6 portions and space them at least 2 inches apart on the baking sheet. Press the biscuit and apple pieces firmly together to create large mounds. Transfer the baking sheet to the middle rack of the oven.

5. Bake for 32 to 37 minutes, until the fritters are a deep golden brown and firm to the touch. Remove the baking sheet from the oven and allow the fritters to cool for 15 to 20 minutes.

6. While the fritters cool, prepare the Basic Vanilla Glaze as indicated on page 60.

7. Dip each fritter in the glaze, flipping to coat both sides. Allow the excess to drip back into the bowl, then transfer the fritters to wire racks. Let the fritters sit for about 20 minutes, or until the glaze has dried.

CHURROS CON CHOCOLATE DONUT HOLES

PREP TIME 25 MINUTES | **BAKE TIME** 20 MINUTES | **INACTIVE TIME** 30 MINUTES

I f you've ever been to Spain, you're likely familiar with *churros con chocolate*—light-as-air pieces of cinnamon-sugared fried dough served with a cup of rich chocolate for dunking. These donut holes with molten chocolate centers channel the Spanish treat into a single bite—no plates or cups needed!

MAKES

●

ABOUT
18 DONUT
HOLES

DONUT MAKER

HOMEMADE
HEAD START

FOR THE CHOCOLATE GANACHE FILLING

3 ounces bittersweet or
   semisweet chocolate,
   finely chopped

2 teaspoons (9g)
   unsalted butter

¼ cup (60ml) heavy cream

FOR THE CHURRO DONUT HOLES

Nonstick cooking spray

3 tablespoons (42g)
   unsalted butter, melted

2 teaspoons (10ml)
   canola oil

6 tablespoons (75g) firmly
   packed light brown sugar

1 large egg, at
   room temperature

½ teaspoon vanilla extract

¼ cup (60g) sour cream,
   at room temperature

¼ cup (60ml) whole milk,
   at room temperature

1 cup plus 2 tablespoons
   (142g) all-purpose flour

¼ teaspoon ground cinnamon

1 teaspoon baking powder

¼ teaspoon baking soda

¼ teaspoon salt

FOR THE CINNAMON-SUGAR COATING

4 tablespoons (57g)
   unsalted butter

½ cup (100g)
   granulated sugar

1 tablespoon ground
   cinnamon

⅛ teaspoon salt

TO MAKE THE CHOCOLATE GANACHE FILLING

1. Place the chocolate and butter in a microwave-safe bowl. Microwave on high for 30 seconds, just until the chocolate appears slightly softened. Add the heavy cream to the bowl, and microwave for 20 to 30 seconds more, until the cream gently bubbles. Remove the bowl from the microwave.

2. Stir gently until the chocolate is fully melted into the cream and the mixture is smooth and glossy. If any pieces of chocolate remain, microwave the bowl in additional 10-second increments, stirring after each time until the chocolate is fully melted and smooth. Set the ganache aside to cool at room temperature while you make the donut holes.

TO MAKE THE CHURRO DONUT HOLES

1. Preheat the oven to 350°F. Spray your donut hole pan with nonstick cooking spray.

2. Place the melted butter, canola oil, brown sugar, egg, vanilla, sour cream, and milk in a large mixing bowl. Whisk until smooth.

3. Add the flour, cinnamon, baking powder, baking soda, and salt to the bowl. Continue whisking until the mixture is combined into a smooth batter.

4. Divide the batter evenly among the prepared donut hole cavities, filling each almost to the top. Transfer the pan to the middle rack of the oven.

5. Bake for 15 to 17 minutes. If using a donut hole maker, follow the manufacturer's instructions. The donuts are done when a toothpick inserted comes out clean.

6. Remove the donut hole pan from the oven and allow the donut holes to cool for 10 minutes in the pan. Carefully remove the donut holes from the pans and transfer them to wire racks to cool completely, about 20 minutes.

CONTINUED ▶▶

CHURROS CON CHOCOLATE DONUT HOLES *CONTINUED*

TO ASSEMBLE THE DONUT HOLES

1. Fit a pastry bag with a small round piping tip and fill the bag ¾ full with the chocolate ganache filling. Use a skewer to poke a hole into each donut hole, stopping about ⅔ deep. Insert the piping tip into the hole and squeeze the bag to fill the donut hole with chocolate. When the donut is full, you will feel a bit of resistance on the tip. Be careful not to fill the hole so much that it splits open. Remove the bag and repeat with the remaining donut holes.

2. Make the cinnamon-sugar coating. Place the butter in a microwave-safe bowl. Microwave on high for 25 to 30 seconds, or until fully melted. Stir together the granulated sugar, cinnamon, and salt in a shallow bowl.

3. Brush each donut hole lightly on all sides with the melted butter. Roll each donut hole through the cinnamon-sugar to fully coat.

INGREDIENT TIP For a Homemade Head Start, replace the chocolate ganache with ½ cup of store-bought hot fudge sauce or Nutella. Warm it in the microwave for 10 to 15 seconds before filling the donut holes.

QUICK AND EASY BEIGNETS

PREP TIME 10 MINUTES | **BAKE TIME** 20 MINUTES | **INACTIVE TIME** 15 MINUTES

One of my culinary dreams is to visit New Orleans. I *love* creole and soul food and often fantasize about the dishes I'd eat during a visit. When I do finally go, my first stop will be for the famous beignets. The French-born pastries are impossibly light on the inside, with crispy exteriors, and are dusted with an unapologetic amount of powdered sugar just before they're served. The idea alone makes my mouth water, so until I find myself down South, I'll keep making this shockingly simple version at home.

MAKES

12 BEIGNETS

_____

HOMEMADE
HEAD START

2 (8-ounce) tubes refrigerated crescent roll dough

½ cup (60g) powdered sugar, for dusting

1. Preheat the oven to 350°F. Line a baking sheet with parchment paper.
2. Carefully remove a sheet of crescent roll dough from its tube and lay it on a flat surface with the long side closest to you. Gently press together the perforations. Fold the sheet of dough in half crosswise so it looks like a card. Take the bottom edge and fold the dough in half once more.
3. Using a rolling pin, gently roll the dough into a roughly 7-by-6-inch rectangle. Cut the rectangle in half once lengthwise and twice crosswise so you have 6 equal pieces. Arrange the pieces 1 inch apart on the baking sheet.
4. Repeat steps 2 and 3 with the second tube of crescent roll dough. Transfer the baking sheet to the middle rack of the oven.
5. Bake for 13 to 16 minutes, until the beignets have puffed up and are a deep golden brown. Remove the baking sheet from the oven and allow the beignets to cool completely, about 15 minutes.
6. Shortly before serving, dust the beignets liberally with powdered sugar using a fine-mesh sieve.

DONUT HOLEMBOUCHE

PREP TIME 45 MINUTES | **BAKE TIME** 20 MINUTES | **INACTIVE TIME** 35 MINUTES

Perhaps you've heard of *croquembouche*, the French dessert made from piling dozens of pastry puffs into a large cone shape with delicate threads of caramelized sugar. A celebratory dessert if there ever was one, it's often served around Christmas, as the cone resembles a decorative tree. It's delicious and impressive but unbelievably time-consuming. Enter the Donut Holembouche, where a mix of donut holes becomes a festive tree with the help of a foam craft cone and toothpicks. Your holiday guests will be in awe of this attention-grabbing work of donut art that's beautiful to look at and fun to eat!

MAKES

1 (8-INCH) TREE (48 TO 60 DONUT HOLES)

1 doubled recipe Old-Fashioned Cake Donuts (page 14) or Cake Mix Donuts (page 26), prepared as donut holes
1 recipe Basic Vanilla Glaze (page 60)

1½ cups (180g) powdered sugar, sifted
Holiday colored nonpareils, for topping
1 bunch fresh rosemary sprigs, for garnish

1. Prepare your choice of donuts as indicated. Be sure to double the recipe and follow the instructions for baking them in donut hole pans. It will take between 4 and 5 dozen donut holes to trim this tree.
2. While the donut holes cool, make the Basic Vanilla Glaze as indicated on page 60. Place the powdered sugar in a separate bowl.
3. Coat one half of the donut holes in powdered sugar and the other half in glaze. Sprinkle nonpareils onto each glazed donut hole immediately after dipping. Allow the donut holes to set for a full 25 minutes before assembling the tree, as the glaze needs to be very dry.

4. To make the tree, set an 8-inch-tall foam cone on a large serving platter. Beginning around the bottom, insert a toothpick into the cone about ½ inch from the bottom, and push it deep enough so only ½ inch of the tooth pick is exposed. Secure a glazed donut hole onto the toothpick. Insert another toothpick ½ inch off to one side of the first donut hole, then secure a sugared donut hole onto it.

5. Repeat until you have a ring of donut holes around the bottom of the cone. Continue working up the tree in concentric circles, alternating glazed and sugared donut holes, until the cone is fully covered. Insert a final toothpick perpendicular to the top of the cone, then secure one last donut hole as the top.

6. To finish your masterpiece, cut or tear the rosemary sprigs into 1- and 2-inch pieces. Tuck the sprig pieces into any exposed spaces between the donut holes. *Très belle!*

COFFEE AND DONUTS TRIFLE

PREP TIME 35 MINUTES | **BAKE TIME** 15 MINUTES | **INACTIVE TIME** 1 HOUR

O ne of my favorite desserts is tiramisu. The traditional Italian dessert consists of espresso and marsala wine–soaked ladyfinger cookies layered with mascarpone custard, and finished with a generous dusting of cocoa powder. This trifle is the easier, Americanized version: coffee-soaked donuts, which can be prepared up to two days in advance, and no-cook espresso cheese-cake mousse alternate in a trifle bowl under a final layer of lightly sweetened whipped cream. Don't be deterred by the various components. This decadent dessert is extremely easy to make, feeds a crowd, and looks stunning when finished.

MAKES

1 (4-QUART) TRIFLE (20 TO 24 SERVINGS)

ADULTS ONLY

1 recipe Old-Fashioned
    Cake Donuts (page 14)

FOR THE COFFEE SOAK

1 cup (250ml) strong
    brewed coffee
2 tablespoons (25g)
    granulated sugar

1 tablespoon (15ml) brandy
    or cognac (optional)

FOR THE ESPRESSO MOUSSE

20 ounces (560g) cream
    cheese, softened
1¼ cups (250g)
    granulated sugar

2 teaspoons instant
    espresso powder
2 teaspoons vanilla extract
4 cups (1,000ml) heavy
    cream, cold

FOR THE WHIPPED CREAM TOPPING

1 cup (250ml) heavy
    cream, cold
2 tablespoons (25g)
    granulated sugar

1 teaspoon vanilla extract
1 tablespoon unsweetened
    cocoa powder, for dusting

Prepare the donuts as indicated on page 14. Once the donuts have cooled, cut or break them into 1-inch pieces and set aside.

TO MAKE THE COFFEE SOAK

Whisk together the brewed coffee, sugar, and brandy (if using) in a measuring cup and set aside.

TO MAKE THE ESPRESSO MOUSSE

1. Place the cream cheese, granulated sugar, espresso powder, and vanilla in a large mixing bowl. Use a hand mixer or stand mixer to beat on medium-high speed for 3 to 4 minutes, until the mixture is completely smooth.

2. Add 1 cup of the heavy cream to the bowl. Beat on low speed to incorporate it into the cream cheese mixture, then add the remaining cream. Turn the mixer to medium-high and beat for 3 to 4 minutes, just until the cream holds stiff peaks. Don't overbeat.

TO MAKE THE WHIPPED CREAM TOPPING

Pour the heavy cream into a separate large bowl. Beat with a hand mixer on medium high for about 3 minutes, until it holds soft peaks. Add the granulated sugar and vanilla and continue beating for 1 to 2 minutes more, until medium-stiff peaks have formed.

TO ASSEMBLE THE TRIFLE

1. Arrange ⅓ of the donut pieces in a 4-quart trifle bowl. Pour ⅓ of the coffee liquid evenly over the donuts. Layer with ½ of the espresso mousse. Top the mousse with another ⅓ of the donuts, followed by ⅓ of the coffee liquid and ½ of the mousse.

CONTINUED ➺

COFFEE AND DONUTS TRIFLE *CONTINUED*

2. Arrange the final ⅓ of the donuts over the mousse and sprinkle with the remaining coffee liquid. Spoon the whipped cream topping onto the donut layer, then use the back of the spoon to spread it to cover the donuts, creating pretty swooshes.

3. Dust the cocoa powder evenly over the whipped cream using a fine-mesh sieve. Refrigerate the trifle for at least 1 hour before serving.

VARIATION TIP For a Mocha Donut Trifle, try using Chocolate Cake Donuts (page 16) instead of Old-Fashioned Cake Donuts.

DONUT BREAD PUDDING WITH VANILLA CUSTARD SAUCE

PREP TIME 15 MINUTES | **BAKE TIME** 1 HOUR | **INACTIVE TIME** 1 HOUR

I hadn't tried bread pudding until my twenties, when I started baking professionally and was asked to develop multiple recipes for different flavored puddings. Now I fully understand its popularity. Not only is it a comforting, soul-warming dessert, it's also an excellent way to repurpose stale bread—or in this case, donuts. This recipe is incredibly versatile: You can use cake donuts or raised donuts, plain, sugared, or glazed. A homemade vanilla custard sauce complements the soft spiced pudding. For an adults-only dessert, spike the sauce and soak the raisins with a touch of bourbon or spiced rum.

MAKES

9 TO 12
SERVINGS

ADULTS ONLY

FOR THE BREAD PUDDING

1 recipe Old-Fashioned
    Cake Donuts (page 14)
¼ cup (41g) raisins
¼ cup (60ml) bourbon or
    spiced rum (optional)
Nonstick cooking spray
3 large eggs
⅔ cup (162ml) heavy cream

1⅔ cups (400ml) whole milk,
    plus more as needed
¼ cup (50g) light
    brown sugar
1½ teaspoons vanilla extract
1½ teaspoons ground
    cinnamon
¼ teaspoon salt

FOR THE VANILLA CUSTARD SAUCE

3 large egg yolks
¼ cup (60ml) heavy cream
¾ cup (180ml) whole milk
Dash of salt
Dash of ground nutmeg

1 teaspoon vanilla extract
2 tablespoons (30ml)
    bourbon or spiced
    rum (optional)

CONTINUED ➡

DONUT BREAD PUDDING WITH VANILLA CUSTARD SAUCE *CONTINUED*

Place the raisins in a small bowl and pour in the bourbon. Cover the bowl and allow the raisins to soak for at least 30 minutes or up to overnight. (If making this recipe without alcohol, simply skip this step.)

TO MAKE THE BREAD PUDDING

1. Preheat the oven to 350°F. Spray a 9-inch square baking dish or pan with nonstick cooking spray.

2. Cut the donuts into 1-inch pieces.

3. Place the eggs, heavy cream, milk, brown sugar, vanilla, cinnamon, and salt in a large mixing bowl. Whisk until the mixture is thoroughly combined.

4. Drain the raisins from the alcohol and scatter them into the bowl. (If not using bourbon, simply add the raisins.) Add the donut pieces to the bowl and toss gently with a rubber spatula until the pieces are evenly coated. The mixture will be quite wet, with a bit of liquid pooled at the bottom of the bowl. If it seems dry, add a few additional tablespoons of milk.

5. Pour the mixture into the prepared baking dish and lightly press it into a mostly even layer. Cover the dish with a sheet of aluminum foil, then transfer it to the middle rack of the oven.

6. Bake for 35 minutes. Remove the foil and continue baking for 20 to 25 minutes longer, until the pudding is golden brown on top and the center is firm to the touch. Remove the dish from the oven and allow it to cool for at least 30 minutes before serving. While the pudding bakes, prepare the vanilla sauce.

TO MAKE THE VANILLA CUSTARD SAUCE

1. Whisk together the egg yolks and heavy cream in a medium saucepan until smooth. Add the milk, salt, and nutmeg, and whisk to combine. Set the saucepan over medium-high heat.

2. Cook, whisking steadily for 5 to 6 minutes, until the sauce starts to bubble and slightly thicken. Once it's bubbling, remove the pan from the heat. Whisk in the vanilla and bourbon or rum (if using). Allow the sauce to cool at room temperature until ready to serve.

3. Donut bread pudding can be served warm or chilled, drizzled with the vanilla sauce. If you don't plan to serve it immediately, refrigerate the sauce in an airtight container. Gently warm it in the microwave for 15 to 20 seconds before serving.

TECHNIQUE TIP This recipe works especially well with donuts that are one to two days old and a bit stale. You can arrange the donuts on a baking sheet and let them dry out in the oven (turned off) or another cool, dry place the day before you plan to make the recipe.

VARIATION TIP Make this with raised donuts—even ones that have been sugared or glazed. Raised donuts will absorb more moisture than cake donuts, so increase the milk to 1¾ cups (437ml) and the heavy cream to ¾ cup (182ml). If using plain donuts that haven't been sugared or glazed, increase the brown sugar to ½ cup (100g).

CHAPTER

7

savory

JALAPEÑO-CHEDDAR CORNBREAD DONUTS

PREP TIME 20 MINUTES | **BAKE TIME** 15 MINUTES | **INACTIVE TIME** 30 MINUTES

I used to live next to a woman in her seventies, and when she learned my career, she asked for a good cornbread recipe. Years later, I still get text messages from her saying, "I lost the cornbread recipe again, can you please resend it?" Each time, she'll send photos back to me, detailing every ingredient she substituted and the results. Her playfulness always makes me laugh, and I can't wait for her to make this recipe for cheesy, slightly sweet, spicy cornbread donuts.

MAKES

12 DONUTS

65 MINI
DONUTS

MAKE IT MINI

ONE BOWL

Nonstick cooking spray
½ cup (115g) unsalted
    butter, melted
¼ cup (50g)
    granulated sugar
2 tablespoons (38g) honey
1 large egg, at
    room temperature
1 cup (250ml) buttermilk,
    at room temperature
1 cup (125g) all-purpose flour

1 cup (120g) fine cornmeal
1 teaspoon baking powder
½ teaspoon baking soda
½ teaspoon salt
¼ teaspoon garlic powder
1 small jalapeño pepper,
    seeded and finely minced
½ cup (4 ounces) finely
    shredded Cheddar
    cheese, divided

1. Preheat the oven to 350°F. Spray your donut pans with nonstick cooking spray.
2. Place the melted butter, sugar, and honey in a large mixing bowl and beat with a hand mixer on medium-high speed for 12 minutes, until smooth and combined. Add the egg and continue beating for 1 minute more, or until the mixture is light and fluffy. Pour in the buttermilk and beat on low for about 30 seconds, until just incorporated.

3. Add the flour, cornmeal, baking powder, baking soda, salt, and garlic powder. Beat the mixture on medium-low speed, scraping down the sides of the bowl with a rubber spatula as needed, until just combined. Fold in the jalapeño and half of the Cheddar cheese.

4. Divide the batter evenly among the prepared cavities. Sprinkle the remaining Cheddar cheese evenly onto the tops of the donuts. Transfer the pans to the middle rack of the oven.

5. Bake for 12 to 14 minutes, or 7 to 8 minutes for mini donuts. The donuts are done when a toothpick inserted comes out clean.

6. Remove the pans from the oven and allow the donuts to cool for 10 minutes. Carefully remove the donuts from the pans and transfer them to wire racks to cool completely, 15 to 20 minutes more.

INGREDIENT TIP Don't care for heat? Substitute the jalapeño pepper with 1 tablespoon finely minced scallion.

GARLIC BREAD PULL-APART DONUTS

PREP TIME 10 MINUTES | **BAKE TIME** 25 MINUTES | **INACTIVE TIME** 10 MINUTES

Just when you thought garlic bread couldn't get any better, it's safe to say pull-apart donuts are the savory, buttery bread's final form. Both fresh garlic and garlic powder flavor these buttery bites, which are almost too easy to make thanks to store-bought bread dough. A sprinkle of Parmesan creates a crisp top crust that will melt in your mouth. Serve these donuts as an appetizer with a bowl of marinara for dipping, or as a side to any Italian-inspired meal.

MAKES

12 DONUTS

HOMEMADE
HEAD START

ONE BOWL

Nonstick cooking spray
½ cup (115g) salted butter, melted and divided
¼ cup grated Parmesan cheese, divided

1 garlic clove, grated
½ teaspoon garlic powder
½ teaspoon dried oregano
2 (11-ounce) tubes French bread dough

1. Preheat the oven to 375°F. Spray your donut pan with non-stick cooking spray.
2. Whisk together half the melted butter, half the Parmesan cheese, the grated garlic, the garlic powder, and the oregano in a large mixing bowl.
3. Remove the French bread dough from the tubes. Cut the dough into 1-inch pieces and place them in the mixing bowl. Toss with a rubber spatula until the pieces are thoroughly coated in garlic butter.
4. With clean hands, arrange the dough pieces in the donut cavities, using roughly the same amount for each donut. The pieces should be packed together fairly tightly but not appear as though they're going to burst from the pan. Transfer the pan to the middle rack of the oven.

5. Bake for 15 minutes. Open the oven and swiftly sprinkle the remaining Parmesan cheese evenly over the donuts. Continue baking for 7 to 10 minutes more, until the donuts are deep golden and sound slightly hollow when tapped.
6. Remove the pan from the oven. Allow the donuts to cool in the pan for 10 minutes, then very carefully remove them and transfer to a serving platter. Brush the remaining melted butter over the donuts and serve immediately.

OLIVE, FIG, AND ROSEMARY DONUTS

PREP TIME 10 MINUTES | **BAKE TIME** 15 MINUTES | **INACTIVE TIME** 30 MINUTES

While the combination of these flavors may be unexpected, the salty olives, sweet dried figs, and earthy rosemary come together in a slightly crumbly donut that's truly irresistible. Make them for a dinner party; and I promise you no one will complain about a basket of donuts on the table instead of rolls. Or prepare them as mini donuts for a unique addition to an antipasto platter.

MAKES

12 DONUTS

65 MINI DONUTS

DONUT MAKER

MAKE IT MINI

ONE BOWL

Nonstick cooking spray
½ cup (115g) unsalted butter, softened
2 tablespoons (25g) light brown sugar
2 large eggs, at room temperature
½ cup (120g) sour cream, at room temperature
¼ cup (60ml) whole milk, at room temperature

1¾ cups (215g) all-purpose flour
1 teaspoon baking powder
½ teaspoon baking soda
½ teaspoon salt
⅓ cup (60g) pitted kalamata olives, minced
⅓ cup (50g) dried figs, minced
1 tablespoon fresh rosemary leaves, finely minced

1. Preheat the oven to 350°F. Spray your donut pans with non-stick cooking spray.
2. Place the butter and sugar in a large mixing bowl and beat with a hand mixer on medium-high speed for 1 to 2 minutes, or until smooth and combined. Add the eggs, sour cream, and milk. Continue beating for 1 minute more, or until the mixture is light and fluffy.

3. Add the flour, baking powder, baking soda, and salt. Beat the mixture on medium-low speed, scraping down the sides of the bowl with a rubber spatula as needed, until just combined. The batter will be thick. Fold in the minced olives, figs, and rosemary.

4. Spoon the batter evenly among the prepared cavities. Use the back of the spoon to smooth the batter out evenly. Transfer the pans to the middle rack of the oven.

5. Bake for 12 to 14 minutes, or 7 to 8 minutes for mini donuts. If using a donut maker, follow the manufacturer's instructions. The donuts are done when a toothpick inserted comes out clean.

6. Remove the pans from the oven and allow the donuts to cool for 10 minutes. Carefully remove the donuts from the pans and transfer them to wire racks to cool completely, 15 to 20 minutes more.

THANKSGIVING STUFFING DONUTS

PREP TIME 15 MINUTES | **BAKE TIME** 25 MINUTES | **INACTIVE TIME** 10 MINUTES

Stuffing is one of the most popular side dishes on the Thanksgiving table, and the best part is the extra-crispy edges along the sides of the pan. This year, to sidestep a race for the best pieces, try baking the stuffing in a donut pan. Every portion will have an equal ratio of crisp to soft pieces—plus, imagine the joy of seeing donuts on a platter next to the turkey! I recommend using day-old Italian bread for the best results.

MAKES

12 DONUTS

HOMEMADE HEAD START

Nonstick cooking spray
12 ounces day-old bread
1 small onion
2 stalks celery
4 or 5 fresh sage leaves
Leaves from 3 or 4 sprigs fresh thyme
Leaves from 1 small sprig fresh rosemary
1 garlic clove
2 tablespoons (28g) unsalted butter
1½ cups (375ml) chicken or vegetable broth
2 large eggs
¾ to 1 teaspoon salt
¼ teaspoon freshly ground black pepper

1. Preheat the oven to 375°F. Spray your donut pan *liberally* with nonstick cooking spray.
2. With a sharp knife, cut the bread into ½-inch cubes and place them in a large mixing bowl. Finely dice the onion and celery. Mince the sage, thyme, rosemary, and garlic.
3. Set a large skillet over medium-high heat and add the butter. Once the butter is melted, add the diced onion and celery. Sauté for 7 to 8 minutes, until the vegetables are softened and translucent. Add the herbs and garlic and cook for about 30 seconds longer, until fragrant.
4. Add the sautéed vegetables and herbs to the bowl of bread cubes. Toss gently to combine.

5. In a separate bowl, whisk together the broth, eggs, ¾ teaspoon of salt, and black pepper. (If using low-sodium broth, increase the salt to 1 teaspoon.) Pour into the bowl of bread cubes and fold gently with a rubber spatula until the bread cubes are evenly moistened.

6. Divide the stuffing evenly among the prepared cavities, and firmly pack it down. Transfer the pan to the middle rack of the oven.

7. Bake for 23 to 25 minutes, until the donuts are deeply browned at the edges and firm to the touch. Remove the pan from the oven and allow the donuts to cool for 10 minutes in the pan.

8. Very carefully remove the donuts from the pan by running the tip of a paring knife around the inner and outer edges. Coax the donuts up and out with either the knife tip or an offset icing spatula. Serve immediately.

TROUBLESHOOTING TIP Be sure to spray your donut pan *very* well with nonstick cooking spray. Otherwise, the stuffing donuts may stick to the pan and break their shape when you try to remove them. If this does happen, don't worry. The extra-crispy edges are still delicious even if broken up and served from a bowl.

ALLERGEN TIP For gluten-free stuffing donuts, use 12 ounces of thick-cut gluten-free sandwich bread. (I love Canyon Bakehouse brand.) Be sure to use vegetable broth instead of chicken broth if you want to keep the donuts vegetarian.

PIZZA DONUTS

PREP TIME 15 MINUTES | **BAKE TIME** 30 MINUTES | **INACTIVE TIME** 20 MINUTES

Delivery-style pizzas, personal pizzas, pizza pockets, and of course those bite-size pizza snacks we all loved as kids—the winner's circle of the frozen food aisle is definitely the pizza section. A few simple ingredients make these pizza donuts a fun, easy recipe for when the slice craving strikes. Customize them with your favorite toppings or swap out the marinara sauce for pesto—you can't go wrong! Unless, of course, you were to mistakenly call them pizza *bagels* . . .

MAKES

12 PIZZA
DONUTS

HOMEMADE
HEAD START

Nonstick cooking spray
1 (14-ounce) tube
   refrigerated pizza dough
½ teaspoon garlic powder
½ cup (4 ounces) pizza sauce
   or smooth marinara sauce
1 cup finely shredded
   mozzarella cheese

½ cup finely chopped
   toppings (such as
   peppers, mushrooms,
   pepperoni, or olives)
1 teaspoon Italian seasoning
2 tablespoons grated
   Parmesan cheese
4 fresh basil leaves, torn

1. Preheat the oven to 400°F. Spray six cavities of your donut pan with nonstick cooking spray.
2. Remove the pizza dough from the tube and unroll it onto a flat surface. Using a pizza cutter or sharp knife, cut the dough into 6 strips, roughly 6 inches long by 2 inches wide.
3. Take one strip of dough and roll it lengthwise so it resembles a thick straw. Form the roll into a ring and pinch the ends tightly together. Fit the ring of dough into a cavity of the donut pan. Repeat with the remaining strips. Transfer the pan to the middle rack of the oven.
4. Bake for 14 to 16 minutes, until the donuts have risen and are lightly golden brown.

5. Remove the pan from the oven and allow the donut crusts to cool for 10 minutes. Carefully remove the donuts from the pans and transfer them to wire racks to cool for 5 to 10 minutes more, until no longer hot to the touch.

6. With a sharp knife, split each donut in half as you would a bagel, and arrange them cut-side up on a baking sheet.

7. Sprinkle the halves with garlic powder. Spoon about 2 teaspoons of pizza sauce around each donut, then use the back of the spoon to gently spread it. Sprinkle each donut with 1 generous tablespoon of shredded mozzarella cheese, and roughly 2 teaspoons of toppings. Transfer the baking sheet to the upper-middle rack of the oven.

8. Bake for 8 to 11 minutes, until the cheese is fully melted and just starting to brown. Remove the baking sheet from the oven. Sprinkle the Italian seasoning and Parmesan cheese evenly over the pizza donuts, top with the basil leaves, and serve immediately.

VARIATION TIP For Pesto Pizza Donuts, substitute ½ cup of prepared basil pesto sauce for the pizza sauce.

EVERYTHING BAGEL DONUT BOMBS

PREP TIME 35 MINUTES | **BAKE TIME** 20 MINUTES | **INACTIVE TIME** 3 HOURS

I met my best friend while auditioning for a televised baking competition in Los Angeles, 600 miles from where we both lived. I'll forever be grateful for how the stars aligned for us; she is the sister I never had and truly the best baker I know. For our many similarities, we have one major difference—I love all sweet baked goods, and she loves savory. I thought a soft everything bagel donut exploding with scallion cream cheese would be her ideal breakfast, so I made it a reality! These are *so* good that even with a sweet tooth as big as mine, I have no self-control when they're on my counter.

MAKES

12 DONUTS

FOR THE BAGEL DONUTS

½ cup (125ml) water

½ cup (125ml) whole milk, plus more as needed

2 teaspoons (7g) active dry yeast

¼ cup (50g) sugar

1 large egg

3½ cups (445g) all-purpose flour, plus more as needed

¼ teaspoon baking soda

1 teaspoon salt

¼ cup (57g) unsalted butter, softened

Nonstick cooking spray

1 large egg white

¼ cup everything bagel seasoning

FOR THE CREAM CHEESE FILLING

8 ounces cream cheese (225g), softened

1 large egg yolk

1 large scallion, green part only, finely minced (optional)

TO MAKE THE BAGEL DONUTS

1. Place the water and milk in a large measuring cup. Microwave for 20 to 30 seconds, until very warm to the touch but not hot. Stir in the yeast.

2. Fit your stand mixer with a dough hook attachment. Pour the yeasted liquid into the stand mixer bowl. Add the sugar and egg. Stir to combine.

3. Add the flour, baking soda, and salt to the bowl. Turn the mixer to medium-low to combine the ingredients. Once the dough begins to come together, increase the mixer speed to medium. With the mixer running, begin adding the butter a spoonful at a time, waiting until each spoonful is mostly incorporated into the dough before adding the next.

4. Once all the butter is added, continue running the mixer until the dough is completely smooth and starts to collect around the dough hook, pulling away from the bottom and sides of the bowl. This may take up to 15 minutes. Scrape down the sides of the bowl with a rubber spatula as needed. The dough will be very tacky. If it appears very wet halfway into kneading, add 1 additional tablespoon of flour. If it appears a bit dry, add a few teaspoons of milk.

5. Spray a large mixing bowl with nonstick cooking spray. Transfer the dough to this bowl using a rubber spatula and clean, slightly dampened hands. Turn the dough to coat it lightly in the nonstick spray. Cover the bowl with a sheet of plastic wrap or a heavy kitchen towel.

6. Place the bowl in a warm area and allow it to proof for 1½ to 2 hours, or until doubled in volume. While the dough proofs, make the cream cheese filling

CONTINUED ➡

EVERYTHING BAGEL DONUT BOMBS *CONTINUED*

TO MAKE THE CREAM CHEESE FILLING

1. Line a large baking sheet with parchment paper. Place the cream cheese in a mixing bowl and beat with a hand mixer on medium-high speed for 2 to 3 minutes, until completely smooth. Add the egg yolk and scallion (if using), and continue to beat 1 minute more, until combined.

2. Divide the mixture into 12 equal mounds on the baking sheet, as you would for drop cookies, using 1 heaping tablespoon for each. Transfer the baking sheet to the freezer for at least 1 hour while the dough continues to proof.

TO MAKE THE DONUT BOMBS

1. Line two large baking sheets with parchment paper. Turn the dough onto a generously floured work surface. Use a rolling pin to very gently roll the dough to a ½-inch thickness. Use a 3-inch circular cutter to stamp out your donuts. Gently collect the dough scraps and reroll them, repeating the cutting process until you have 12 rounds.

2. Remove the baking sheet with the cream cheese filling from the freezer. Take a round of dough and gently roll it to be just under ¼ inch thick. Place a frozen cream cheese mound in the center of the round, then collect the edges of the dough to encompass the mound, pinching the dough together to fully seal the seams. Place the donut bomb seam-side down onto a baking sheet. Repeat with the remaining dough and filling.

3. Spray the donut bombs with nonstick cooking spray and cover them loosely with plastic wrap or a clean kitchen towel. Allow the donuts to proof again for 30 to 45 minutes, or until they appear puffy. Preheat the oven to 350°F in the last 15 to 20 minutes of proofing.

4. Shortly before baking, brush the tops of the donut bombs with the egg white. Sprinkle the everything bagel seasoning generously onto the tops of the donut bombs. Transfer the baking sheets to the middle rack of the oven.

5. Bake for 16 to 18 minutes, until the tops of the donut bombs are deep golden and they sound slightly hollow when tapped. Remove the baking sheets from the oven and allow the donut bombs to cool for at least 20 minutes before serving.

INGREDIENT TIP Everything bagel seasoning can be found along with the spices in most grocery stores. Trader Joe's sells it for only $2 a bottle! For a homemade version, combine 1 tablespoon white sesame seeds, 1 tablespoon black sesame seeds, 1 tablespoon poppyseeds, 2 teaspoons minced dried garlic, 2 teaspoons minced dried onion, and 1 teaspoon flakey/coarse sea salt.

DOGGIE DONUTS

PREP TIME 10 MINUTES | **BAKE TIME** 15 MINUTES | **INACTIVE TIME** 30 MINUTES

Imagine if you had to spend your entire life watching everyone around you eat donuts but were never allowed to try one yourself. This is a dog's reality, and it is no way for any good boy or girl to live. I developed this recipe specifically for our four-legged friends, using simple pantry ingredients you likely already have on hand. These donuts have passed many rounds of quality control by expert testers, all of whom have agreed that the bacon garnish makes them look extra fetching.

MAKES

8 DONUTS

45 MINI
DONUTS

DONUT MAKER

MAKE IT MINI

Nonstick cooking spray
½ cup (125g) pumpkin puree
¼ cup (64g) smooth peanut butter
1 large egg
¾ cup (185ml) milk (whole or skim)

1 cup plus 2 tablespoons (140g) whole-wheat flour (or all-purpose)
1 teaspoon baking powder
½ teaspoon baking soda
4 strips cooked bacon (optional)

1. Preheat the oven to 350°F. Spray your donut pan with non-stick cooking spray.
2. Place the pumpkin puree, peanut butter, and egg in a large mixing bowl and whisk until smooth. Add the milk and whisk to combine.
3. Add the flour, baking powder, and baking soda to the bowl. Continue whisking until the mixture is combined into a smooth batter.
4. Divide the batter evenly among the prepared cavities. Transfer the pan to the middle rack of the oven.
5. Bake for 12 to 14 minutes for regular donuts, or 7 to 8 minutes for mini donuts. If using a donut maker, follow the manufacturer's instructions. The donuts are done when a toothpick inserted comes out clean.

6. Remove the donut pan from the oven and allow the donuts to cool for 10 minutes in the pan. Carefully remove the donuts from the pan and transfer them to wire racks to cool completely, about 20 minutes. Tear the bacon strips in half crosswise and lay one half on each donut, if desired.

INGREDIENT TIP The bacon makes a fun garnish, but you can also finely chop it and fold it into the donut batter before baking, or leave it out entirely. Whatever your pup prefers!

RESOURCES

Here are my recommendations for specific equipment and ingredients. They can be found at your local grocery or baking supply store or online.

- **Standard Donut Pans:** A standard-size donut pan with 3½-inch cavities is the one thing you truly need. I've used Wilton's 2-pack of 6-cavity nonstick donut pans to bake *thousands* of donuts over the past few years.

- **Mini Donut Pans:** I use the Wilton 12-cavity mini donut pan to make mini donuts. On some sites, it's called the "medium" donut pan. Just look for the one with 1¾-inch cavities.

- **Donut Hole Pan:** Donut holes are a treat no one can pass up, and they're especially fun to make with kids. I have Wilton's 20-cavity non-stick donut hole pan, and love it.

- **Donut Cutter:** The Ateco 3½-inch stainless steel donut cutter can make yeast donuts easier by cutting the outer and inner rings in a single motion.

- **Food Coloring:** I prefer quality gel food coloring to the liquid dyes.

The colors look more natural and vibrant, and the pigments are stronger, so you'll use less for each batch of icing. A 12-color set of Wilton's gel-based icing colors can create endless possibilities and will last you a long time.

- **Gluten-Free Baking Flour:** Bob's Red Mill Gluten-Free 1-to-1 Baking Flour is a blend of different gluten-free grains and starches designed specifically for baking. It can be used cup-for-cup in place of traditional flour to make almost any donut gluten-free. This particular blend is my favorite, as I think it best approximates the texture of wheat flour.

- **Kitchen Scale:** A kitchen scale is invaluable to any baker. I've been using my Ozeri ZK14 digital scale, which comes in a bunch of fun colors, for years!

RECIPES BY OCCASION

INDEX

ACKNOWLEDGMENTS

You know what they say: It takes a village to bake a donut. Dozens of people played roles in the successful writing, editing, and testing of this book.

To Grandma Joan and Haji, who selflessly allowed me to develop nearly 75 percent of the recipes from their home kitchen, never once commenting on the powdered sugar fingerprints I surely left behind.

To Joe, for fielding incessant donut inquiries and offering valuable chef insight.

To Melissa, Darrell, Valerie, Ryan, Daniel, Amanda, and Anil, for being the best family of foodie friends a baker could ever have. To Greta, for being the best musical friend and keeping my gluten-free recipes sharp.

To Mavish, Kouign of Carbs, who probably didn't sign up to be a 24/7 baking and emotional support hotline but whose aggressive positivity makes all of life, the good and not-as-good, even better.

To my mom and dad, for supplying the Dunkin' throughout my childhood and steadfastly encouraging my creative career path, which can only be described as a parent's worst nightmare. I value your support, love, and advice more than I could ever express in words.

To Callisto Media—Vanessa, who took an unsolicited email from a baker with a donutty passion and somehow made it into a book. Sam, for curating such drool-worthy donut imagery. And Gleni, for working editing magic on every word in less time than it takes an oven to preheat.

Lastly, to the countless people who helped eat all these donuts while listening to me talk ceaselessly about donuts for two months straight, thank you. Though I guess it's hard to talk back when you have a donut in your mouth.

ABOUT THE AUTHOR

SARA MELLAS is a culinary creative working as a recipe developer, cookbook author, and food stylist for a wide variety of clients. Holding advanced degrees in music history, opera, and education, Sara worked professionally as a conductor and music teacher for many years, while spending every spare moment of time in the kitchen. She is an overcompetitive baker, most recently winning the 2018 Kellogg's Holiday Baking Championship and the 2019 Guittard Chocolate Passion Contest.

Sara's approach to food is fresh, colorful, and a little whimsical, with a focus on whole ingredients and seasonality. She strives to create reliable recipes for bakers and cooks of all skill levels, with results as delicious to eat as they are beautiful to look at. When not in the kitchen or doing something musical, Sara enjoys training for NPC physique competitions and riding horses. Sara lives in Nashville, Tennessee, with her one-year-old oven and three-year-old stand mixer.

For more of Sara's work, visit www.saramellas.com, and follow along on Instagram at @sara.mellas.